Guide to Overcoming Anxiety

Written by **Charlie Wardle**

First published 2020

Published under licence by Brown Dog Books and
The Self-Publishing Partnership Ltd, 10b Greenway Farm, nr. Bath BS30 5RL

www.selfpublishingpartnership.co.uk

ISBN printed book: 978-1-83952-158-4
ISBN e-book: 978-1-83952-159-1

Cover design by Kevin Rylands
Internal design by Andrew Easton

Printed and bound in the UK
This book is printed on FSC certified paper

MIX
Paper from responsible sources
FSC® C013604

A Practical Guide to Overcoming Anxiety

Written by **Charlie Wardle**
Founder of Climb Your Mountain (CYM)

CLIMB YOUR MOUNTAIN

Table of Contents

A word from the author...

Wouldn't it be nice if there was a magic wand or a magic pill that could instantly make you feel happier and not be anxious? Unfortunately, there isn't, but then again if there was, that wouldn't be as interesting or rewarding as understanding and then overcoming anxiety for yourself!

Many people will experience anxiety in its various forms and for many reasons, yet most will never really understand why. They won't know why they feel, think and behave the way they do, or what are the reasons and triggers for anxiety. But you can! And with the knowledge and understanding and the control that brings, you can overcome your anxiety forever.

I strongly believe that everybody can beat anxiety if they have the understanding and the tools and techniques necessary to manage and prevent it – but that isn't easy and sometimes you need a helping hand, and I am here to give you that hand. But before I do, let's go back to what I need from you throughout this book:

Effort – You get out what you put in. So live, breathe and embrace this book over the next eight chapters – you will see the rewards.

Patience – As the saying goes, a little patience goes a long way.

You may start feeling improvements from day one; you may not realise them until towards the end. But either way, if you have the patience and perseverance, you will get there.

Practice – Practice makes perfect and it is key to overcoming anxiety. Practise the techniques throughout the course in order to reinforce the thoughts, beliefs and actions. The more you practise, the easier it becomes and the greater the results.

Desire – I already know you want this because you've got this far. If you have the desire you will get the results. So never forget why you turned to this book in the first place. You can overcome anxiety and think how much better your life will be in the future.

I know you won't need it, but good luck! If you get stuck, have questions, want to provide feedback or just want to let me know how you are getting on, contact me by email at info@climbyourmountain.org

I wish you the very best. Now go for it!

Charlie Wardle
Founder of Climb Your Mountain (CYM)
www.climbyourmountain.org

How to Use This Book

This book has eight chapters and you should aim to commit to all eight of them.

Anxiety can be very difficult to deal with, and the thought of overcoming it is an exciting prospect, but rushing through the book quickly may mean that you don't gain the full benefit of the information, exercises, and time to think and reflect.

I also know that life is busy and can get in the way, but dedicating a few hours per week to reading the content and a few minutes a day to practising the exercises means that you will have every chance to overcome anxiety and significantly improve your life as a result.

The book has lots of questions, exercises and reflection time, as well as information. Make sure you complete all of these and give the exercises your all. Be honest with yourself and your answers – if this means that you'd rather not write something down, that is fine as long as you are truthful with yourself.

Take your time to really think about any questions posed and your answers, and although it is very much about your own thoughts, it may be useful to ask a close friend, partner or family member their thoughts, so that you can gain a different perspective. You never know, their answers might surprise you.

Spread your weekly commitment to this book however best works for you, but commit yourself to making that time and make that commitment now. You already know this but it will be reiterated throughout the next eight chapters that the more you put in, the more you get out. The effort will be rewarded and the more you learn, understand, apply and practise, the more your confidence will grow and skills develop to overcome your anxiety once and for all.

Each chapter starts with the objectives and before you proceed onto the following one make sure that you feel you have fulfilled those objectives. If you cannot do this it may be that you need to complete the exercises or that you need more time to absorb the information presented. Don't worry if this is you; some chapters will be harder than others.

If you do get stuck please feel free to contact me on info@ climbyourmountain.org or proceed to the next chapter, but make a note to return to that pending objective later on.

Introduction

Everyone will feel anxious from time to time. It is a normal and natural reaction to certain situations and it can be a good thing as it may help us focus and concentrate more, and protect us. However, for a lot of people anxiety can be a very negative experience and cause many unnecessary issues in their lives.

There are many different types of anxiety disorder and the degree to which it can affect us will vary considerably. It is the most common mental health condition, with around 25% of people experiencing what could be diagnosed as anxiety disorder during their lives, and many millions of people experiencing the condition in any given year.

As we will see, there are all kinds of effects and costs to individuals as a result of anxiety, and furthermore, many others will also be directly or indirectly affected. This can include partners, family members, children, parents, work colleagues, employers, etc. Anxiety can really damage and affect our relationships, our friendships, our family, our health, and our happiness.

Additionally, there is a huge cost to society in increased healthcare costs, medication costs, reduced productivity, time off from work, costs to business, plus possible knock-on effects like alcohol, drug, and substance abuse issues. It is a major issue for individuals, families, communities, public health, and society as a whole, and much more should be done to educate and inform people, so there is more understanding, which means it is more likely to be managed and overcome.

Some typical examples of when someone may experience increased levels of anxiety are shown below. Some level of anxiety is normal but if the feelings are higher than what is considered normal then issues can result and it is important to understand more about why you feel this way and the damaging effects it can have.

- Sitting a test or an exam
- Going to the dentist
- Waiting on health test results
- Going to hospital
- Flying
- Attending an interview
- Starting a new job
- Going on a date
- Doing a presentation or group talk
- Moving away from home
- Having a baby
- Being diagnosed with an illness
- Paying bills and other money issues
- Starting a new relationship
- Deciding to get married or divorced

For people suffering from anxiety disorder, almost anything outside of their normal routines will create feelings of anxiety.

Give the next eight chapters everything you have and you will be able to overcome your anxiety and be able to lead a much happier life.

Special section – Coronavirus impact

In this updated edition of the book, I thought I should write a new section relating to the coronavirus impact and how it has affected anxiety. I am currently writing this in mid-April 2020, so we are 3–4 weeks into the 'lockdown'.

You probably first heard about the virus sometime in late-January or early February 2020, and as time went on over the next few weeks the information we had and the potential issues arising started to escalate, though it wasn't until later in March that most people really started to be fully aware of how serious and unprecedented this virus was going to be. One of the main factors in increased anxiety is uncertainty and the unknown – this virus and the consequences of it were very much uncertain and unknown – thus people's anxiety levels were naturally raised significantly. People who already had anxiety were getting worse and many people who had not previously been anxious were experiencing these feelings and thoughts for the first time. Anxiety amongst society was and presumably still is increasing as a result.

However, it is not all doom and gloom with regard to anxiety. Certainly in the short term it is a real concern but out of every difficult and negative situation, I firmly believe there can be positives. Firstly, I want to offer some advice which I hope will help anyone with anxiety to both reduce and manage their situation (and indeed help others to do the same) but additionally, I want to look at some of the real positives that could be achieved from this.

Flatten the curve

All of us would have heard the government and the scientists talk about 'flattening the curve' with regard to the coronavirus and more specifically the rate of infection, cases, hospitalisation and deaths. Essentially, by reducing the transmission of the disease we can flatten the curve to manageable levels, and although still very damaging, we can as a society lower the damage. In many ways this principle can be used in relation to your anxiety levels – you want to flatten your own curve to lower your anxiety levels and lessen the damage this situation could cause you.

So by thinking in these terms you can make the necessary and effective steps to lower your anxiety levels as much as possible and then eventually be in control and ultimately overcome your anxiety just as we will overcome the coronavirus.

Everything is temporary

It is so important to remember that everything is temporary – both the bad stuff and the good stuff. At times when things are going well, you must try to recognise and appreciate this and not take things for granted or become complacent. However, when going through the bad times, it is also essential to remember it won't last forever and things will improve and become good again – don't lose faith.

The same goes for this situation with the coronavirus, as it won't last forever and it is only temporary. I don't know when you are reading this (and hopefully things have greatly improved since the time of writing) but things will definitely improve, there will be more certainty and knowledge, and people's lives, in general, will improve. It may take some time but the terrible situation and effects we have seen will be temporary.

Lack of Control & Uncertainty

Probably the biggest factor that causes increased anxiety is a lack of control and uncertainty in your life, and with the coronavirus, for a number of reasons, there is a huge amount of uncertainty and a lack of control with the situation both for individuals and our society as a whole.

However, it is really important to focus on what you can control and try not to think too much about what you cannot control. Of course, that is difficult when there is so much uncertainty and lack of control – but if you focus your efforts and time on what you are able to control, it will really help you. Write down things that you can and can't control in your life and then focus on all those things you can control and have much more certainty about and it will really help during these periods.

Rational thoughts and facts

It is so important to remain as rational as possible in everything you do and think. The more rational you are, the easier it will be to reduce and manage your anxiety. Make sure, wherever possible, you have the facts and make your own judgements based on these, rather than hearsay or other people's opinions. There is so much misinformation, lies, hidden agendas, mistakes, conspiracy theories and other stuff that is not helpful and will only increase anxiety. So make sure you listen to good, unbiased sources of information and try to limit the amount of time spent listening to the news or opinions on what is or isn't happening.

If you find your anxiety building up and worrying about various issues, take a step back and try to rationalise the situation and your thoughts. And remember things will improve and probably all the things you may currently be worrying about will soon not be an issue.

Focus on positives

It is always important to remain positive in any situation and to focus on the positive things. It may feel at times, especially now, that there are no positives to focus on, but there always are! Again, it can be useful to write things down, so why not make a list of all the things that are positive, both in your life and in society as a whole.

By taking time to think and consider the positives, you will reduce anxiety levels and be more optimistic, which in turn leads to more positive thoughts and actions. You could also ask friends or family members to tell you about the positive things they can think of as they may have ones you haven't thought of and vice versa. Positive thinking really does make a difference and it is something you can control.

Set small goals each day

To give you some focus and to help you remain productive, I would suggest setting some small goals each day. Perhaps think about five things you can do the next day which will be helpful, productive and positive and write them down. For example, clean the car, cut the grass, go for a run, clean the bathroom, read a book, have a bath, call a friend, tidy the garage, listen to some music, write a poem, bake a cake or do some yoga. The five goals can be anything and could be trying something new, as long as they are productive and achievable and it will help you pass the time in a helpful way. And don't forget to praise yourself once you have completed them!

Productive v Unproductive

One of my main mantras is to be as productive as possible in everything you do (and think). It can only be beneficial for you if most of what you do is productive, as opposed to unproductive, and if you are honest with yourself, you will know whether what you are doing or thinking is productive or not.

So whenever you find yourself doing or thinking stuff that is unproductive, and therefore not helpful to your situation, then stop, rethink and start again in a productive way. The more you recognise this and practise, the easier it becomes and the more benefit you get, including reducing your anxiety levels.

The good news!

In every bad situation and negative experience, there can always also be positives and good news. At times it may be difficult to see these, but there are positives both for yourself and others. With the coronavirus, although terrible, there have been so many uplifting and positive stories, whether that is the amazing work by so many people, the volunteers, the fundraising efforts, etc plus the positive impact on the environment and an opportunity to reassess many things in our lives and reflect on our priorities individually and as a society.

The selfless acts, the inspiring stories, the heroic efforts should not be forgotten and the opportunities we have had to try new things, learn about ourselves, reflect on our lives, understand more about who we are and what is important. And also remembering that at these times it is so important to have hope and to know that we will get through this and things will improve.

As an example of something I had never done before, I decided to write a poem and here it is!

At these times

Everything has changed in our world that we know, can we recover from this terrible low?
You may feel lost with a sense that you're sinking, with so much uncertainty and negative thinking.
When will it all end, you keep asking when? At these times, will it ever be normal again?
So much disruption, discomfort and stress, how can we ever get out of this mess?

Things are difficult and it is a real struggle, and at these times you may just want a cuddle.
That might not be possible, which, of course, is a shame, but sadly the situation isn't a game.
Yet, although loved ones may be apart, you know they are still with you, deep in your heart.
And we know that if we all come together, this situation, well, it won't last forever.

Look out for each other, go check on a neighbour, or if out and about then smile at a stranger.
And whenever you can, make sure that you talk, and get outside for your once-daily walk.
Glance up to the stars and look for the moon, and make sure you listen to your favourite tune.
Even though you may be stuck in a room, at these times, you could try using zoom.

Special Section

We do what we can and obey all the laws, thus saving lives and stay home indoors.
But we're in strange times with no kids at school, though some may think that's actually quite cool.
Others, sadly, might have had nightmares, but at these times as we come down the stairs
There's PE with Joe first thing in the morning, before the 'fun' of the parental homeschooling.

There are wonderful things to be thankful for, like the inspirational Captain Tom Moore.
The doctors, nurses, carers and key workers, the Nightingale hospitals with help from the Gurkhas.
So many heroes, like a true band of brothers, at these times, we know there are many others.
Too many to mention, the list is much longer, but coming together, to make us all stronger.

We can all play our part and step up to the plate, keep doing the right things, it's never too late.
Although it's not over, there's still a mountain to climb, we will get through this most difficult time.
We all have to look out for the light ahead, and stay strong for each other until this virus is dead.
And remember this, when it's so hard to cope, at these times, we still always have hope.

Chapter 1

What is Anxiety?

Objectives:
During this first chapter we want to understand what anxiety actually is, looking at the symptoms and the different types of anxiety there are and starting to focus on your own anxiety issues.

What is Anxiety?

'A feeling of worry, nervousness or unease about something with an uncertain outcome.'

Anxiety is the name that covers several disorders that can cause nervousness, apprehension, worry and fear. These disorders affect our thinking, feelings and behaviours, and they can also cause physical symptoms. There is a wide spectrum of anxiety issues, from mild anxiety – which is still unpleasant and unsettling – through to severe anxiety – which can be extremely debilitating – having a very serious impact on daily life for the person and people around them.

How would you define anxiety and how would you explain and describe your anxiety? Please write your thoughts down in this box:

At a general level, anxiety can be broken down into two areas:

Real-time anxiety and Anticipatory anxiety

Real-time anxiety is essentially the anxiety someone experiences physically, in real time, when they are actually in an anxiety-causing situation or event. For example, when they are on a plane, or they see a spider, or are delivering a speech, or walking in the dark, or driving in heavy traffic, etc. It means the event is actually happening now and the anxiety is happening during the event. It happens there and then in the moment and there may not have been any build-up, as the person may not have been expecting it.

Anticipatory anxiety is essentially the thinking, worrying, or brooding about certain expected events that the person views as stressful, dangerous, threatening or challenging. For example, worrying about a flight they are taking next week, a dentist's appointment next month, delivering a presentation at work in the near future, or driving a long journey at the weekend. They are anxious about a future event which they imagine will be difficult, scary and unpleasant, and by thinking about it they are magnifying the fear and the thoughts, and the anxiety worsens. There are several common examples of how people 'think anxiously', which provide reasons for problems and also cause additional problems. Here are some of the main ones which may resonate with you:

Racing thoughts

Consistently thinking and overthinking, with negative thoughts and worry, in an uncontrollable way. An inability to switch your mind off or relax, with all the racing thoughts going on.

Poor concentration

When you find yourself unable to concentrate on things or focus your thoughts. Your attention span is limited and your short-term memory may be affected.

Approval addiction

When you find yourself worrying about what other people think of you and needing their approval. The more anxious you are, the more likely this is to occur.

Worst-case future

When you think about the future but focus on all the things that may go wrong and how things could turn out in a negative way, effectively looking at the worst-case scenarios rather than reality.

Magnification

When you make more of things in a negative way than they actually are, which could be past events, current situations or future happenings. Magnifying their importance in a negative and unhelpful way.

Perfectionism

When you want everything to be perfect, and when it is not, focusing on all the negatives and assuming anything that isn't perfect is a mistake or a failure, compounding your anxiety.

Take some time to think if any of the above 'think anxiously' examples apply to you.

Symptoms of Anxiety

There are a whole range of symptoms, experiences, characteristics, behaviours, thoughts, reactions and sensations related to anxiety. It is probably easier to focus on these by splitting them into physical and psychological sensations. Although not an exhaustive list, this shows the wide range of different effects that anxiety can produce, and in an ideal world you wouldn't be experiencing any of them.

Physical sensations:

- Nausea (feeling or actually being sick)
- Tense muscles and headaches
- Burping and increased digestive acid reflux
- Pins and needles, particularly in the arms
- Feeling light-headed or dizzy
- Feeling too cold or too hot
- Faster breathing
- Sweating or hot flushes, including night sweats
- A fast, thumping or irregular heartbeat
- Raised blood pressure
- Difficulty sleeping
- Needing the toilet more frequently, or less frequently
- Churning in the pit of your stomach
- Experiencing panic attacks

Psychological sensations:

- Feeling tense, nervous and on edge
- Having a sense of dread, or fearing the worst
- Feeling like the world is speeding up or slowing down
- Feeling like other people can see you're anxious and are looking at you

- Feeling your mind is really busy with thoughts
- Dwelling on negative experiences, or thinking over a situation again and again (this is called rumination)
- Feeling restless and not being able to concentrate
- Feeling numb

Think about your anxiety and specific examples of when you are most anxious and what happens to you in these situations. Write some examples down in the table below:

Examples of what you get anxious about	What are your symptoms?
e.g. I really hate flying	I can't sleep for days before a flight, my heart races, I can't focus on anything, I sweat more

What type of anxiety is it?

Modern life – Increased levels of Anxiety

Levels of diagnosed anxiety have been increasing over the last few decades and there are several important factors to explain this. No doubt one of these is that there is more understanding: people are becoming more aware of this issue and are therefore more likely to seek help, go to a doctor, and be diagnosed. There is also the increasing lack of exercise and increasingly unhealthy food and drink consumption that also can contribute to increased anxiety levels.

However, something else that plays a very big part in anxiety is the way we live our lives in the modern world. There are so many examples of modern life that can be factors in the increasing levels of anxiety for many people. Our lives tend to be faster-paced, busier, with more expectations and pressures, increased stresses, comparisons, connections, and of course there is social media.

Social media with the likes of Facebook, Twitter, Snapchat, WhatsApp, Instagram, etc. means we are exposed to so much information about other people's lives that this tends to put greater expectations on our own lives to fit in, be popular, respond to stuff, as well as making more comparisons which leads to assumptions about our lives and other people's. All of this can lead to increased anxiety if not managed effectively.

There is also the media in general, which tends to sensationalise news, events and stories and increase fear and worries. We receive so much more information than in past times, via new media, and much more negative information. There is the constant news about terrorism, crime, violence, lack of security, natural disasters, disease and illness, etc., which can also heighten anxiety levels because we can magnify the dangers and real threats to us from these reported situations.

There are many wonderful benefits of technology and the modern world, but there are also more opportunities for people to become anxious about the increased information available and for this problem to outweigh the good things. So be careful, be aware of the downsides, don't compare so much, get things in perspective where possible, and embrace the good whilst limiting the bad.

WhatsApp & Texting example

There are many examples of how modern technology and advances have improved our lives, but also many examples where they have created problems and increased anxiety, worry and paranoia. You may not necessarily be aware of this upcoming example, or it may not be something that affects you; however, it is a good example that many people can relate to it.

WhatsApp is a modern messaging tool many people use on their phone to communicate with people including friends, family and partners. One of its features is the ability to see if another person is online, when they were last online and if they have read your message (unless you switch this option off, but then that in itself raises suspicions!). For many people, when they send a text to someone, they are anticipating a reply and the wait for a response can raise anxiety.

Anxiety levels can be further increased if you know that the other person has seen your text or message or is online. Questions you may find yourself asking in your head could include:

- Why don't they reply? They must have seen the message.
- What are they doing?
- Who else are they communicating with?
- Why were they online at that time?
- Why does it take them so long to respond?
- Why are they not online?
- Why are they not using their phone?
- Are they with someone else?

So many potential assumptions can be reached, usually in a negative, worrying and paranoid way that causes increased anxiety and makes the situation worse, especially if it relates to a partner or potential partner – raising important trust issues and insecurities. Overthinking, paranoid thoughts, worst-case scenarios, unhelpful assumptions all come to the fore. It is possible your assumptions are correct but more likely there are explanations that wouldn't be an issue. For example, they are driving so can't respond, they are in a meeting, on the landline phone, talking to a family member, a best friend, a work-related issue or simply they can't get a signal.

So many arguments, stresses, paranoid thinking and increased anxiety can result from modern texting/messaging methods which didn't exist a few years ago. Be aware of the potential issues and be careful not to make too many assumptions too quickly. And of course, texting/messaging in itself is not a great way to communicate as often things will get misinterpreted or lost in translation. So be very aware how bad texting can be for so many reasons. Face-to-face communication is best if possible.

'Texting is a brilliant way to miscommunicate how you feel
and misinterpret what other people mean.'

Different types of Anxiety Disorders

There are several different types of anxiety that can be identified and diagnosed, and it is important to distinguish between them, so that you can understand the types and differences in order to best deal with the issues.

In some cases the symptoms are very similar, or it can be a combination of different types. Here are the most common forms of anxiety disorders:

Generalised Anxiety Disorder

Generalised Anxiety Disorder (GAD) is a chronic disorder characterised by excessive, long-lasting anxiety (several months or more) and worry about non-specific life events, objects and situations. It is the most common type of anxiety disorder and is more prevalent amongst young adults and women, although it can affect anyone.

GAD sufferers often feel afraid and worry about health, money, family, work or school, but they have trouble both identifying the specific fear and controlling the worries. Their fear is usually unrealistic or out of proportion with what may be expected in their situation. Sufferers expect failure and disaster to the point that it interferes with daily functions like work, school, social activities and relationships.

Social Anxiety

Social Anxiety Disorder is a type of social phobia characterised by a fear of being negatively judged by others or of public embarrassment due to impulsive actions. This includes feelings such as stage fright, a fear of intimacy, and a fear of humiliation. This disorder can cause people to avoid public situations and human contact to the point that normal life is rendered very difficult or impossible.

Agoraphobia

Agoraphobia is an anxiety disorder characterised by anxiety in situations where the sufferer perceives certain environments as dangerous or uncomfortable, often due to the environment's vast openness or crowdedness. These situations or environments include wide-open spaces and crowded places, as well as uncontrollable social situations such as the possibility of being met in shopping centres and airports, and on bridges. The sufferer may go to great lengths to avoid those situations and in severe cases become unable to leave their home or safe haven.

Obsessive-Compulsive Disorder

Obsessive-Compulsive Disorder (OCD) is an anxiety disorder characterised by thoughts or actions that are repetitive, distressing and intrusive. OCD sufferers usually know that their compulsions are unreasonable or irrational, but they serve to hopefully alleviate their anxiety. Often the logic of someone with OCD will appear superstitious, such as an insistence in walking in a certain pattern. OCD sufferers may obsessively clean personal items or hands or constantly check locks, stoves or light switches. OCD may also take a more deceptive form: for example, having to visit the gym a certain number of times a week. OCD is a very time-consuming and preoccupying disorder because it leads to rituals that must be followed before or during the achievement of the activity of daily life.

Post-Traumatic Stress Disorder

Post-Traumatic Stress Disorder or Syndrome (PTSD) is a psychological reaction to a highly stressful event outside the range of everyday experience, such as military combat, terrorist attack, physical violence, or a natural disaster. The symptoms usually include depression, anxiety, flashbacks, recurrent nightmares, and avoidance of situations that might trigger memories of the event. If you develop strong feelings of anxiety after experiencing or witnessing something you found very traumatic, you might be given a diagnosis of PTSD. PTSD can cause flashbacks or nightmares, which make you feel like you're reliving all the fear and anxiety you experienced during the actual event.

Phobias

A phobia is an irrational fear and avoidance of an object or situation. Phobias are different from generalised anxiety disorders because a phobia has a fear response identified with a specific cause. The fear may be acknowledged as irrational or unnecessary, but the person is still unable to control the anxiety that results. Stimuli for phobia may be as varied as situations, animals or everyday objects. For example, agoraphobia occurs when one avoids a place or situation to avoid an anxiety or panic attack. Agoraphobics will situate themselves so that escape will not be difficult or embarrassing and they will change their behaviour to reduce anxiety about being able to escape.

Panic Attacks

Panic attacks, or panic disorders, are brief but sudden attacks of intense terror and apprehension that include difficulty breathing, dizziness, shaking, confusion, nausea, and an overwhelming sense of not being in control. Panic attacks can arise out of the blue, with little build-up, but although they usually peak after no more than 10 minutes, they then may last for hours in some shape or form. Panic disorders can occur after frightening experiences or prolonged stress, or they can occur spontaneously, and although there will be underlying reasons, any number of triggers can set them off. In addition, panic attacks often lead a sufferer to expect future attacks, which may then cause drastic behavioural changes in order to avoid these attacks.

Here is a description from someone who has suffered from panic attacks:

"It's like the world is getting smaller, noises are more enhanced; rushing in your ears, things start to swim. It gets harder to breathe. It's emotional, like a tight band round your head, overwhelming feelings of dread. Then

maybe lashing out verbally, physically, and emotionally, gasping for breath, tears, tight chest, heart pounding and feeling out of control and a sense of fear. Afterwards there is embarrassment, still feeling on edge, feeling very emotional, still fear and a feeling of failure.

Advice I would give: You're not the only one to have them. Take deep breaths, focus on a given point, and try to relax. If I feel the start of one, where possible I try to remove myself from the situation – or just work through it, know that it is happening, and accept it. It will be ok."

Body Dysmorphic Disorder

Body dysmorphic disorder (BDD) is an anxiety disorder relating to body-image. If you have BDD you experience concerns about your appearance that cause you significant anxiety and have a disruptive effect on your life. You may also develop routines and habits, such as excessive use of mirrors or picking your skin, to deal with the worries you have about the way you look. These habits usually have a significant impact on your ability to carry on with your day-to-day life.

Health Anxiety

When experiencing health anxiety disorder you believe that the physical and psychological symptoms you are experiencing are due to some life-threatening health condition which has not been diagnosed. As a result you spend time obsessed with health conditions and their negative consequences. You become very sensitive to the normal functioning of your body and frequently 'scan' your body for symptoms. You will also want to visit health practitioners regularly because you believe they will have the answers to your condition and to confirm your beliefs. However, this in turn can increase anxiety and frustrations if and when there is no diagnosis.

Creating your Counter-Anxiety Toolbox

Many people do, and will, suffer from anxiety. Indeed, as many as one in four people will be directly affected with anxiety and therefore it stands to reason that pretty much everyone will be affected indirectly as they will know somebody (a partner, a friend, a family member, or a colleague) where anxiety really affects their life.

There are many types of anxiety and many factors that can cause it, as we have seen. One of the most common aggravating factors is negative thinking. Negative thinking causes more negative thinking and thinking in a negative way compounds the anxious thoughts. It becomes a vicious circle whereby the more anxious you are, the more negative thinking results, and the more negative thinking, the more anxious you become.

Of course the answer is to stop thinking negatively. However, anyone who has any experience of anxiety knows full well that it is virtually impossible to just 'snap out' of it. It is easy to quickly compound an anxious thought and build up the anxiety even more, and very quickly you can get into what I would call an 'anxiety mountain' where you quickly build layers of further anxiety, which then build higher and higher. It is not nice, but there seems to be only one direction to go and that is a larger anxiety mountain and the higher you build this mountain, the more difficult it is to deal with.

There is hope, though, and a way of managing this, which in time will become very effective, and although it may not in itself treat the anxiety, it can certainly manage it and allow you to lead a much more normal, positive, happier life. What you need to do in the first place is recognise these negative thoughts and stop that anxiety mountain building and taking effect.

The idea is that whenever you start to think negatively or something happens to set you back and put you into a negative mindset, then you recognise this, log it, and take action by going to your toolbox. Your personal toolbox is one that we will develop together and tailor to what works best for you. It is important to understand that everyone is different and therefore something that works well for someone else may not necessarily work for you.

The toolbox is designed to be a collection of practical applications that you can go to at any time to find something appropriate that will stop the spiral of decline and pull you back upwards before negative thinking manifests itself into more negative thinking. The more options you have in the toolbox, the more likely you will be able to find something that works quickly and effectively in any given situation.

Imagine a real toolbox with a variety of tools that are each different but all have their own uses. If you just had screwdrivers or hammers or wrenches then your toolbox isn't going to be the saviour of the day in all situations. But if you had a full spectrum of tools, then the chances are you will have something there to fix whatever problem arises.

Some examples of what could your toolbox	feel free to add some more be in of your own
-Listen to some favourite music -Go outside for a walk -Have a long, hot shower -Arrange to meet a friend for a coffee -Go to the cinema and watch a film -Cook yourself a healthy meal -Have a good tidy up and clean the house -Write down a list of productive things to do -Set some goals and focus on how you will achieve them -Do some gardening -Read some inspiring quotes -Identify some new hobbies or skills to learn -Go to the gym or try a new exercise class -Read some books or do some of your own research -Watch some funny clips on YouTube -Take a short break somewhere for a day or two -Try writing some poetry -Think about doing a charity fundraising event	

CHAPTER 1 SUMMARY

There has been a lot of information to digest but this will provide greater understanding to leave you better placed to deal with and overcome your own anxiety. The more knowledge you have then the more control you will have and the better the tools and techniques you can develop to help you. Make sure you have completed the questions and exercises and start using the toolbox on a daily basis. The more practical tools you have to use in any given situation the better you will be able to cope and manage your thoughts.

Well done on completing the first chapter – remember it will take time and effort but you are already making really good positive steps.

Chapter 2
Causes, Reasons & Understanding Yourself

Objectives:
This chapter we will focus on the potential causes and reasons for anxiety. We also look to understand more about why you feel anxious by understanding yourself better. By doing this you will feel more in control and the anxiety you have will make more sense providing a better foundation to overcome it effectively.

Causes & Reasons for Anxiety

Underlying reasons:

There can be a wide range of causes and reasons why people develop anxiety issues, and generally it is a combination of genetics, upbringing, education, general and specific experiences, and habit. The more you can understand about what your causes and reasons are, the better you will be placed to manage, reduce and prevent any anxiety issues.

Genetics

When we are born we inherit our genetics and DNA and we have no say in the matter. However, our genes play a big role in who we are, how we behave, what we do, what we think, what we look like, and how we live our lives. Anxiety can be caused by many factors, including our genetics, and they will always play some part in any issues we experience.

Upbringing

Our upbringing, and particularly our early childhood, has a huge impact on who we are and shaping the type of person we become. Usually our parents are the main influences during our upbringing and many underlying anxiety issues will form during this period of our lives. It may not be anyone's fault, especially yours, but it is important to understand that what you experienced and how you were influenced during your upbringing is likely to play a big role in any issues you later have in your life.

Education

In addition to your upbringing, the education you have and your school experiences are likely to have an impact and be an underlying factor in any anxiety problems. The standard of education, the teachers, your friends and classmates, potential bullying, social interaction, performance, praise, reward, and perceived success or failure can all be factors.

General and specific experiences

Undoubtedly a huge factor in any anxiety-related issues we may have come about as a result of our life experiences. This will include both good and bad general experiences, as well as specific events that occur during our lives. Particularly bad, difficult, challenging, and traumatic experiences will impact on our future thoughts and behaviours and how we think about and react to things.

Experiences that have previously caused worry, concern and anxiety are likely to cause similar feelings unless they are dealt with, understood and overcome effectively. So it is really important to tackle issues at the time so that they are less likely to affect you again in the future.

Hormones & brain chemistry

Our physiological make-up, including our hormones and brain chemistry, can play a part in our anxiety levels, both directly and indirectly. The neurotransmitter levels in our brains will influence how we feel, and our mood, which in turn will impact on our anxiety as well as hormone levels associated with our thyroid and pituitary glands, and these can affect everyone.

Furthermore, for women in particular, both the monthly menstrual cycle and the menopause can have a direct and indirect influence on anxiety and associated issues. Physical and emotional changes occur that can cause additional stress, increased worry, and anxiety levels due to hormones.

Habit

Although any form of anxiety can cause problems and have a detrimental effect on your life, it is also possible that the anxiety you have can become effectively a habit. Humans are habitual creatures and when you get used to something and keep doing it, or it is a constant factor, then it is far more likely to remain. Many people with anxiety will become used to it, expect the feelings and behaviours that occur, and in a strange way they may potentially be comforted by this. It becomes part of them and who they are and they can't imagine it being any different.

On the basis that we become what we constantly do, anxiety can become a habit, and this may prevent the person from actually facing up to the issues and working on understanding them. If they don't look to understand, act, and resolve, then the anxiety is much more likely to remain. Do not let your anxiety become a habit. Do not just accept this is part of you and what you have. You can overcome, manage and deal with any anxiety issues and as a result your life will be better, healthier and happier.

Specific Reasons:

The most common specific reasons that cause anxiety are shown below, but the effect they have on an individual will vary considerably and can change depending on many other contributing factors.

Financial issues

Usually identified as the most common cause of stress and anxiety in the UK, financial issues can affect anyone, although it tends to decline with age. Especially in recent years, with the huge increase in consumer debt, access to credit and loans, the recession, job insecurity, and cost of living increases, the levels of financial problems and associated anxiety have increased. There is also quite a low level of financial education, with many people not understanding enough about money, savings, debt, costs, income, rates, credit, etc. This means that many people don't know how best to deal with financial problems, which further increases anxiety, and they may be too scared to confront the issues and so the problem remains or worsens, as do the stress, worry and anxiety. It is so important to be honest about money problems and seek appropriate advice and help in order to deal with the issues, otherwise additional health problems will arise as well as the financial ones. For example, you could use the advice on the MoneySavingExpert.com website, and similar sites, or speak to friends or family members who may have good financial knowledge and experience, or go to a finance professional.

Relationships

Relationships are a common cause of anxiety, both when in a relationship and when single. Many people will feel anxious and even experience a type of stigma associated with being single. They may desire to be in a relationship, so when this isn't the case they may become anxious as to when it might happen, who with, why are they single, what is wrong with them, how can they meet someone, what if they remain single and alone, etc. Many negative and anxious thoughts can build up, although this tends to be more to do with underlying insecurities and low confidence levels, rather than actually being single.

When in a relationship there are many examples of how anxiety can develop. Is this relationship working, can I trust them, what are they doing, who are they texting, do I want children, should we move in together, do I love them, do they love me, why don't they call me, do they find me attractive, we don't seem to communicate, other people seem happier, should I end it, I can't live without them, etc. So many possibilities of how anxiety levels can increase and cause problems within a relationship.

Work and career

For many people their work, job, and career are important to them and as a result this can often cause anxiety issues. Do they enjoy their job, is it secure, what do they really want to do, pressures to achieve, issues with work colleagues and bosses, threat of redundancy, being unemployed, applying for roles, job interviews, career progression, relocation, qualifications, presentations, deadlines, etc. are all examples of potential stresses, worries, and anxiety problems.

Especially as work can be such a big part of your life, there is a lot of potential for this to cause anxiety issues so it is really important to reduce the risk of problems developing and seek appropriate advice if this area of your life is causing concern. There may not be instant solutions but you can manage and reduce anxiety so that it doesn't cause additional stress.

Getting old and death

The fear of getting old and the fear of dying are also quite common reasons for anxiety and can affect people of any age. The thought of feeling and looking old, not being able to do things you enjoy, not being active, getting ill, not being independent, getting wrinkles, losing your hair, life passing you by, not achieving your goals, etc. are all examples of anxiety related to getting old.

The thought and fear of death also raise additional worries such as, I don't want to die, what happens when I die, who will look after my children, there is so much I still want to do, life is too short, what about my family, etc.

Getting old and dying are inevitable, but worrying about it and increasing anxiety will not help or be beneficial in any way. Live your life, embrace it, look after your health, and the rest will look after itself.

Loneliness

Feeling lonely and isolated is also a common reason for anxiety and perhaps surprisingly affects younger people more than older people. Feeling that you are alone, with nobody to talk to or to spend time with, or you don't fit in, or nobody cares about you, and spending much of your time by yourself not out of choice are examples of loneliness.

Humans by nature are social creatures, who also need purpose and fulfilment in their lives, plus they like to love and care, and be loved and cared about, and so if this isn't the case then issues can arise. It can be difficult to get out of the situation and the increasing anxiety makes it more likely to stay isolated and shut yourself away with those feelings without actually addressing them.

Welfare of loved ones

Often anxiety can develop as a result of caring for and being concerned for the welfare of others, particularly loved ones and especially your children.

Whether they are happy or not, illnesses and injuries they may suffer, what are they up to, are you doing the right things for them, will they be ok, are they in danger, who else will look after them if you can't, etc. are all possible factors in this type of anxiety and worry.

You may feel responsible for their lives, you may not have the control you would like, you may feel helpless or ineffective, you may become paranoid about what could happen to them, you may try to empathise by make worrying assumptions, or you may feel guilty about certain events or situations. Generally the anxiety comes from caring, which is a good thing, but it can become a burden that develops negative thoughts and increases unhelpful anxiety issues.

Body-image

The way you look and how you see yourself physically can often lead to anxiety issues, primarily as a result of comparing yourself to others and worrying about what other people will think of you. This can affect anyone, both men and women, though it tends to be more likely amongst younger people. There can be a wide range of body-image anxiety issues, and in more serious cases this can lead to conditions such as anorexia and bulimia.

You may be concerned about specific features like your nose, hair, teeth, legs, feet, tummy, etc., or it could be more general issues of weight, size and proportions. Many aspects of your life will be affected by this and as well as increased anxiety it is likely your confidence and self-esteem will be lower as a result. You may avoid certain events, places or situations, like the swimming pool or beach. You may also get anxious with physical contact or avoid intimacy and sexual activity as a result.

List some examples of your anxiety	Can you identify the potential cause or reason for this anxiety?

Understanding yourself more

What is normal and what is not?

Unfortunately in life we will often encounter setbacks, receive bad news, find ourselves in negative situations, witness unfairness and injustice, and generally have things go wrong and experience things that upset us and cause problems for us. Often they are unpredictable and come out of nowhere, and sometimes they are a slow build-up or a combination of factors. Life will always present problems to everyone at different points in their life, and to varying degrees. But it is important to understand the difference between a 'normal' and 'natural' reaction to such events and circumstances and what could be defined or diagnosed as something more.

If you receive some bad news or a situation occurs that is upsetting, you will have a natural reaction to that. It isn't pleasant and it may take a bit of time to deal with it and overcome it, but that would be normal.

For example, if you went for a new job or a promotion and didn't get it you would be disappointed and upset for a while, or if your pet cat or

dog died you would be very sad and grieving for the loss. These are expected, normal reactions to something negative. However, if you were unable to get over these incidents and the negative thoughts associated continued for a long time and you were preoccupied with worry, stress, and angst related to the situation and couldn't move on, then this could be seen as a problem and not 'normal'.

How to understand yourself

It is very important to try and understand as much as possible about yourself, how you deal with things, how you feel, why you behave a certain way, why you react, why you think the way you do, and what is best for yourself. You need to be responsible and accountable for yourself, and the more you understand, the better position you will be in to prevent problems, manage issues, and overcome the challenges you face. Everyone is different, so you are the best-placed person to really know and understand yourself. As Aristotle said, 'Knowing yourself is the beginning of all wisdom'.

However, understanding and knowing yourself can be much more difficult than it sounds and often requires a lot of work, effort and time. Just because something works for somebody else that doesn't mean it is right for you. Although it is good to seek advice, you need to be conscious that people are different, circumstances are different, and usually people giving advice don't know all the factors or have all the necessary information or knowledge. You are best placed to understand yourself.

Take time to get to know yourself, try to understand your characteristics, behaviours and personality. Do research, gain knowledge, seek feedback, ask for advice, listen to others, reflect on situations and experiences, learn from mistakes, think about your strengths and weaknesses, and find out who you really are. The more you know yourself, the better you will be able to advise yourself and communicate to others so they can understand and advise more appropriately.

Do this exercise whereby you write down how you feel about yourself and your characteristics, identifying both the positive and good things about you and also the negative things. Include your strengths and weaknesses. Take some time to think about this and be honest with yourself. Then ask a close friend or family member for their view on you in the same way. It is a good exercise to reflect and see what you think of yourself and to see how someone else views you.

	Your opinion of you	A close friend or family members' opinion of you
Positives		
Negatives		

Another good exercise to do is think about and write down your current thoughts about the following eight areas of your life so you can identify some key areas of 'good' things in your life and also those areas where you currently feel negative about.

Area of your life	Write down all the positive thoughts you have about each of these areas of your life	Write down all the negative thought you have about each of these areas of your life
Family		
Partner		
Work		
Health		
Money		
Time		
You		
Friends		

From the above exercise are there any particular areas that stand out in relation to your anxiety? For example, is your health a big anxiety issue? Or money? Look to identify any specific areas where there are more clearly issues. Also, where there are areas that you don't feel anxiety issues exist, ask yourself why this is the case and identify why that is so. For example, have you had positive experiences, do you feel secure, are you confident in these particular areas?

Now write down in the box below all the factors that you have identified that make you **not** feel anxious:

You and Confidence

You must look carefully at yourself and your understanding of confidence in relation to anxiety. Think about who you are, your values, your strengths, your weaknesses, your personality, your beliefs, your perceptions, your skills, your thoughts and your behaviours. Be reflective, patient and honest with yourself, but realise you are the most important person in your life, and as two famous sayings state, "it's not the mountain we conquer, but ourselves" and "no one can make you feel inferior without your consent".

What do you think about yourself?

The most important factor affecting your confidence is what you think about yourself. These thoughts will be based on a wide mix of factors including your genetics, your upbringing, your family, people who have influenced your life (in both good and bad ways), your friends, your job, your health, your looks, your body, your experiences (both positive and negative), and much more. Often what you think about yourself will be very different from how other people view you and, although you should know yourself better than anyone, your views of yourself could be influenced by many external factors and may be distorted as a result.

There is a great quote that goes, "**Whether you think you can, or you think you can't, you will most likely be right,**" and in a way this is the same when you think about yourself. Confidence is ultimately how you think or feel about yourself, so in order to be more confident and feel confident you must be able to think positively about yourself and work at being a 'better' you from your own perspective.

Your perception on things, beliefs, thoughts

Although basing things on facts is very important, and wherever possible you should base decisions, thoughts, behaviours and actions on facts, the reality is that your confidence is based upon your perception of things and not always based on facts. So your perception of yourself, of others, of experiences, of information, etc. is key to your confidence.

You should aim to close the gap between perception and facts where you can, but this is not always possible and also can be very difficult. Try to be rational and reflective and consider all factors. Not everything you hear, see or believe will be true, and be careful not to jump to conclusions, or make too many assumptions or judgements without being certain they are correct.

Self-assurance, self-esteem, self-confidence

How self-assured are you? How would you rate your self-esteem? How would you describe your self-confidence? It is important to think about this but ask yourself how you are personally measuring this. What are your criteria? What are you basing your views on? Are you comparing yourself against others and if so, who? Have you always felt like this or are you comparing yourself to the past? If you feel differently now to times in the past then what has changed? What are the factors and reasons? By asking yourself these questions and thinking about them, you are more likely to have a more complete and balanced view and an improved awareness of the factors that have shaped your opinions.

Your attitude, your past, your understanding

Experiences throughout your life will shape your views and so will your understanding of these experiences and your attitude. Many events, situations, people, and circumstances will have contributed to who you are, how you think, how you behave, and how you feel about yourself, which of course impacts on your confidence. By understanding the impact they have had on you, then your ability to deal with them, will play a key role in both how you currently feel and how you can move forward with developing your confidence.

Your attitude is key, too, and this needs to be looked at in detail. Do you want to improve? Do you believe you can improve? Are you willing to make the effort and changes needed to have a more confident and happier life? By wanting to complete this book you have acknowledged some of your anxiety issues and related problems, but you are now on the way to greatly improving your life.

'A bird sitting on a tree is never afraid of the branch breaking, because its trust is not on the branch but on its own wings.'

CHAPTER 2 SUMMARY

There are many potential causes and reasons for anxiety and you will now have identified more clearly the issues you have and the factors that are most influential for you. Reflecting on your life, and understanding who you are and why certain things affect you are really important, so make sure you have taken the time to do this. There is often a close relationship between confidence and anxiety, so understanding your own confidence and building this can have a significant benefit in your goal of overcoming anxiety.

At times it will be tough and can be upsetting to go deep into your life and any issues you are facing, but it is necessary in order for you to have a much happier and anxiety-free future.

Chapter 3
It's All in the Mind

Objectives:
This chapter is focused on understanding more about how your brain works and your thought-processes with the help of 'the Chimp Paradox'. We also look at other key factors in your life that have a major influence and impact on your anxiety levels.

The Chimp Paradox

Chimp paradox overview

A book (also available as an audiobook) that I would strongly recommend is *The Chimp Paradox* by Dr Steve Peters. He is best known for being the team psychiatrist for British Cycling and Team Sky, helping the likes of Sir Chris Hoy, Sir Bradley Wiggins and Victoria Pendleton. The book is described as a mind-management plan and tries to explain the different way the brain works based on neuroscience principles. This in turn helps explain the different thoughts and behaviours we have. By understanding why we think and behave in certain ways it is then possible to be more in control of our thoughts and behaviours in order to reduce any anxiety and increase our confidence, happiness and success.

I will try and explain the basics of the book and hopefully this will be helpful; however, reading The Chimp Paradox in full is advised for a clearer insight.

In simple terms, the brain is divided into three areas that Dr Peters describes as the Computer, the Human and the Chimp, which are all very different.

Starting with the Computer, this is the part of the brain that is full of experiences and memories built up throughout your whole life and will include both good and bad experiences. Nearly every thought and subsequent action will be based in some way on your past experiences and therefore it is important to understand the significance of those experiences and that you can change how they affect you in a positive way. If you have had bad experiences in your life, then it is likely that they will continue to have a detrimental effect on you long after the actual experience. You may not be aware of or realise the damaging effect they can have, but these 'gremlins' are likely always to be there unless you can address them by recognising them, understanding them, and then getting rid of them!

Example of a gremlin

Imagine being a 10-year-old at school. When the teacher asked a question of his pupils you put your hand up and answered in front of the class. However, you misheard the question and your answer was very wrong. But worse than that you had simply given a wrong answer was that the rest of the children started laughing out loud, and even the teacher laughed at you. You felt incredibly embarrassed and upset and that feeling haunted you for ages. Ever since you have become reluctant to speak out, answer questions, put your view across, for fear of this embarrassment happening again. You continue throughout your life being very wary and reluctant to speak up, and your confidence is affected as a result.

Now let's look at this rationally and see if we can get rid of this gremlin.

- Firstly, we all make mistakes and get things wrong.
- Secondly, you were only 10 years old and the children who laughed were only 10 years old – you would have probably done the same.
- Thirdly, you misheard the question, which wasn't your fault.

- Finally, it was just one incident when you were very young. You cannot let this affect you anymore. Acknowledge it happened and then rationally dispose of this gremlin. That situation will not happen again, so speak up, answer questions and you will regain confidence in this area.

Hopefully you will also have had good experiences and these are likely to continue to play a positive role in your life. Of course, the more positive experiences, the better, and it is important to recognise these as well as recognising the negative gremlins. The positive experiences are referred to as 'Auto-Pilots' and the aim is to increase the number of these by generating new positive experiences and also changing some of the bad experiences into positive ones, which can be possible.

The Human part of the brain is the real you and when this is active and working well then we are rational, logical, calm and mature, and our thoughts and behaviours are based upon facts and our core values. This is how we would want to behave most of the time and how we would want other people to behave. The Human part of the brain has developed over hundreds of thousands of years and distinguishes us from other animals. Humans need purpose and fulfilment in their lives.

The Chimp part of the brain is at the core; it is the original part of the brain that existed before the Human part developed and grew through evolution. When this part of the brain is active our behaviour can be very 'unhuman' and our behaviours and thoughts are very much how we might expect a Chimp to be. They will be very emotive, reactive and impulsive, the main instinct being survival, with the options of fight, flight or freeze. So in this mood with the Chimp in control we can be aggressive, excitable, anxious, scared, naughty, etc. We are not rational, we don't look at the facts, we are not logical and we are not mature.

Example of Chimp and Human behaviour

Let's imagine that you are going to an important meeting scheduled for 2pm, and it is normally a thirty-minute drive or less to get to the location of the meeting. You decide to leave at 1.15pm to give yourself plenty of extra time to get there for 2pm. However, on the way there is some unexpected traffic, a combination of roadworks, temporary traffic lights, and a broken-down car. You start to feel agitated and annoyed, especially as nobody seems to be doing any actual roadworks and you expect it was the person's fault who broke down, causing the additional delay. You have given yourself some extra time, though, so you should still make the meeting on time. Once you are clear of the roadworks and traffic lights you then get stuck behind a really slow car and are not able to overtake. Your frustration builds and you become angrier and even more annoyed. You start to think you are going to be late for your important meeting.

Still stuck behind the slow car you decide to try a shortcut and drive through a housing estate, but quite soon, with lots of cars parked on the road, you have to stop to let an oncoming car go by. You stop and wait and let the car go by, but they do not wave to say thank you or acknowledge you in any way and you are outraged. You get so angry that you are fit to explode. You can no longer concentrate on the meeting because you are so worked up that you are late and people are so rude and you finally arrive still angry, upset and agitated.

It is clear that you have been in Chimp behaviour mode. As a result of events and other people's actions out of your control you have let your Chimp take over and make matters worse for you. You are upset and angry, and potentially the important meeting is compromised as a result. Now, if you were able to manage the Chimp and have the Human remain in control you would be in a much better position.

Alternatively, you could consider that you did allow plenty of extra time to get to the meeting, that what happened was out of your control and that you are not to blame. You reflect that there are always 'inconsiderate' drivers out there but you cannot do anything about that. You would rationalise that the best thing for you would be to stay calm, not get upset, let it go, reassure yourself that it's not the end of the world, and gain some perspective on the situation. You would apologise for being a few minutes late and explain the new traffic lights and roadworks, and remain in the right mood and frame of mind for the important meeting.

The Human remains rational, calm and logical whilst the Chimp gets agitated, angry, upset, emotional and reactive. In this situation it is clear that it is better for you for the Human to be in control and for the Chimp to be managed.

The important first step is to recognise when you are thinking and behaving in Chimp mode. If you ask yourself the question or reflect on the situation it will be fairly obvious whether you are in Human or Chimp mode. If you then recognise you are indeed in Chimp mode then you have to work out how best to manage this and how to put the Human back in control. If the Chimp's behaviour and thinking are around anger and aggression, then it may be best to allow the Chimp to have a short outburst but then quickly put him away in a cage to calm down. If the behaviour and thinking are more about being worried, anxious, and scared, then it may be best to reassure your Chimp, give him or her a hug, providing protection and security.

Here is a simple chart explaining some of the key differences between the Human and the Chimp:

	HUMAN	CHIMP
Behaviours	Logical Rational Level-headed Gets the Facts Mature	Reactive Irrational Emotional Excitable Anxious Aggressive
Life is all about...	Purpose Fulfilment	Survival

Life is not fair!

The Chimp Paradox also makes the very valid, if rather annoying, point that life is not fair. In fact it positions this statement as 'the number one rule.' It is really important to understand and accept that life is not fair. Things will happen all the time that are not fair and if you always work on the basis that everything should be fair then you are likely to struggle as a result. Of course we want things to be fair and our own values and morals and beliefs should be based on fairness and not be compromised because life is not fair, however, we must learn to deal with the simple fact that life is not fair and things will happen (in a good and a bad way) to show this all the time.

Your Stone of Life

Something else the book talks about that is really important is your 'stone of life', which is essentially all about your own personal values, beliefs and integrity. It's who you really are as a person and this is important for two reasons.

Firstly, you are who you are. Your values and beliefs are who you are, what you are about and how you go about things in your life. What you do, what you think, how you behave, how you react, how things affect you, etc. are all based on who you are and your stone of life, so you need to recognise and understand this and be aware of your own stone of life.

Secondly, the further away you go from your stone of life, the worse things generally will be for you because you are not being yourself. Whether you realise this or not, it is likely to be detrimental to you if you stray from who you really are and your stone of life. It is often all too easy to be influenced by others and move away from your stone of life and not be the real you, losing your identity, your values, and your integrity. The more this happens the more likely problems will arise. In short, the stone is the foundation for your life, your life should be built upon the stone, not upon the sands of influence or fashion. So understand who you are, work out what your stone of life is, and do your best to stay with it. Be who you are, be consistent to your own values, don't be negatively influenced and don't stray from your stone of life.

Identifying and managing the Chimp!

Practise identifying your Chimp and Human behaviour and also other people's. Every day you will find yourself both in Chimp mode and in Human mode – when you make a concerted effort to recognise your behaviour it is usually very clear what mode you are in.

When you find yourself in Chimp mode try to understand why – Ask yourself these questions:

- What events, actions, people, circumstances, etc. have made you act, think and behave in Chimp mode?
- Has being in Chimp mode helped you?
- Has it made things better for you?
- Do you regret anything you did or said whilst in Chimp mode?

Developing techniques to manage the Chimp and allow the Human to take over:

Step 1 – You have to first recognise you are in Chimp mode

Step 2 – Remind yourself that in most cases being in Chimp mode will not be beneficial for you

Step 3 – Try to take a step back or a deep breath and think what a mature adult human would most likely do in that situation

Step 4 – Think how best to manage the Chimp in that particular situation: for example, does it need reassurance? Does it need to let off steam? Does it need to be put in a cage?

Step 5 – Remind yourself again that you are the Human and can manage the situation and take control of the Chimp

Chimp Mode examples	Human Mode examples

Write down some examples of when you are in Chimp Mode and Human mode – what do you do or say?

Other People

You will always be influenced by other people in life, in both good ways and bad. You cannot control other people, but you can control the effect they have on you and how you think about, and behave towards, others.

With the right people and the right attitude your confidence will increase and your anxiety will reduce significantly. The hard part is ensuring you have the right people in your life and how you deal with, and react to, all of the people that enter your life at different times.

'No one can make you feel inferior without your consent.'
– Eleanor Roosevelt

Why do you worry what people think?

Pretty much everyone, to some extent, worries about what other people think of them. So if you are someone who worries what people think then you are not alone, and to some degree it can be a good thing that you care what others do think about you. However, far too often the worrying about what people think can be damaging, negative and stressful. It will very often lower confidence, cause anxiety and restrict you from doing things, and can lead to health issues.

Worrying that people might not like you, might think you are stupid, might laugh at you, might reject you, etc. are all common and negative concerns which can be detrimental to your confidence.

Do they really think that of you? Would you think like that of others?

Most of the time, our concerns and worries of what others are thinking are simply not a reality. Are people really judging you as you believe they are? Are they hoping to dislike you or laugh at you? Are they willing you to do something stupid or fail? Are they thinking how much better they are than you? Most of the time the answer is definitely no. People you don't really know are normally not that interested, and those people you know as friends or family are going to be supportive and be thinking positively and encouraging you.

When you see or meet people for the first time, are you looking to put them down, laugh at them, dislike them, think they are stupid, etc.? Think about situations where you worry what people are thinking and turn it around to see how you would be thinking in that situation. Would you be so harsh and critical? I suspect the answer is no, and that is how most people will be and if they're not, then is that the type of person whose opinion you want to value anyway?

Other people have issues, problems, insecurities, etc.

It is very easy to focus just on yourself and any particular issues, worries, insecurities, doubts and low confidence you may be experiencing. However, other people have these, too. Yes, you are not the only one who worries and thinks and behaves your way. Many people will be struggling with worse issues and disorders that affect their behaviour and thinking. So be mindful that other people have issues and what you see and get may be down to that. For example, if someone is a bit cold and distant with you upon meeting you, and you take that to mean they don't like you and it must be something bad about you, then consider it could be that they are nervous, lacking confidence, worried about things, introverted, etc.; a whole range of possibilities in addition to the one you are focusing on.

Also, many of the most seemingly confident people are very insecure – with low confidence, low self-esteem and high anxiety – but they cover it up, or their way of dealing with it is to put on the front you see. Never judge a book by its cover.

Why let people cause you negativity, put you down, make you feel worse?

A lot of issues people have with confidence will come either directly or indirectly from other people. So often there will be people in your life, past and present, who will be a negative influence, will put you down, will make you feel worse, and will be chipping away at your confidence and self-esteem. They could be partners, family members, work colleagues, or so-called friends. Sometimes you will be aware of who they are and what they are doing but sometimes you may not even realise unless you actually step back and reflect on things, and by then the damage has been done, the arrow has found its mark. The answer is to stop this happening, either by removing them from your life or by confronting them. However, this can be very difficult and especially difficult if you are struggling with a lack of confidence. Think how you can minimise the negative impact others are having on you. Can you ignore them, can you confront them, could you take them out of your life? Can you be strong enough to acknowledge their opinion but not let it affect you? The more you can minimise the damage caused to you, the better.

'There comes a time when you have to stop crossing oceans for the people who wouldn't even jump puddles for you.'

Security

Feeling secure in your life is a nice, comforting feeling to have and will inherently add to your confidence, just as insecurity will decrease your confidence. People will look at security in a number of different ways and will often get things out of perspective. Think about what security means to you and how you can feel more secure about your surroundings and circumstances, and, most importantly, feel secure within yourself.

Not just about what we don't have – but what we do have

It is all too easy to dwell on what we don't have in life, and many people are constantly thinking about what they would like to have. Ruminating on the things we don't have and the things we want to have can be very negative and very unproductive. It is far better and more productive to think about the positives of what you do have. You will have a lot more than you realise and spending time thinking about all the good things you have will help put things into perspective and likely give you some additional assurance and security. Make a list of the positive attributes in your life and remind yourself frequently about the things that make you smile.

Money, job, partner, family, house, health

It is common for people to focus on particular elements of security, like financial security, and not consider other important areas. Security could be with your job, your partner, your family, your house, your health, and many other things. Would you prefer financial security but poor health and no family? Do you underestimate the security your partner gives you, or that of owning your own property? There are probably areas that do provide you with security, but you rarely think about them, and instead focus on the negative areas that make you feel insecure.

Be realistic about the situation and get things in perspective

It is really important to get life into perspective and be realistic. Understand the real difference between 'need' and 'want' and the reasons behind them. Do not neglect all the positives that can provide security and all of the opportunities to come which will bring greater security for you. Remember, things could always be worse, so count your blessings and be careful not to get things out of perspective.

Being secure in yourself is most important

You have to feel secure in yourself and believe in yourself. Security provides confidence, and in turn confidence helps make you feel more secure, so belief in yourself is key. Strip away the negative thinking, the jealousy, the comparisons, the focus on what you don't have, and instead concentrate on all the positive things you have and all the good things in your life. The more you focus on the positives, the more you will gain belief in yourself and you will look forward and gain momentum in that belief.

'Too many people overvalue what they are not and don't have, and undervalue what they are and do have.'

Having read the above information, now list those positive areas of your life that also bring you security
e.g. I have a good family around me who are supportive, and I know they are there for me

Fears and Worries

As humans we are born with only two fears: the fear of falling and the fear of loud noise. So, apart from these, all our fears that we have are learned fears, either through someone telling us we should be fearful, or from negative experiences that have affected and influenced us.

Fear of failure and fear of rejection

Two of the most common fears we have are the fear of failure and the fear of rejection, which are often closely linked. Nobody likes to fail or be rejected, but why do we fear and worry about these so much? The reality is that everyone will fail and be rejected at times during their life. It will happen. So rather than worrying and being fearful we should accept the inevitable and focus on how we deal with it. How can we learn, understand, grow, become stronger, change if necessary, and use the experience in a positive way? The more confident you are, the less you fear failure and rejection because you are confident that you can deal with the outcome. That is the difference and that should be where the focus is – on how you deal with it, rather than the fear beforehand.

Fear of feeling stupid

Another common fear is that you will do or say something that makes you look stupid. People worry that they won't be able to do something, or not do it correctly, or embarrass themselves in some way. Again, the reality is that we all make mistakes, we all do things that will make us look stupid, and nobody is perfect.

Of course, you can try to minimise the risk in a number of ways, but if you simply stop doing things or saying things because of this fear then you will deprive yourself of so many things and so many opportunities in life. Your confidence will most likely decrease further as you stop being involved, withdraw more from conversations, events and activities and thus deny yourself the experiences that will help increase your confidence. Learn to laugh at yourself if you do say or do something stupid! Accept that you will make mistakes; be honest and humble enough to apologise if needed and accept that you will, on occasion, look foolish, because that is life.

Fear of what others think

A basic human characteristic is the desire and need to be liked and loved. To feel wanted, to feel support and security, to feel that people care, and to feel you have some kind of purpose. Humans are inherently social creatures and like to have contact with others and belong to groups. These basic characteristics tend to make us care about what others think of us so we want to look good and be well thought of by others. It is normal to care about this and to think about it, but this does not mean you should be in fear and constantly worrying about what others think. There is a big difference between being self-aware and caring about something, and being in fear.

Nervous, anxious, scared

It is likely that the lower your confidence, the more nervous, anxious and scared you will feel in various situations. In turn the more you feel like this, the lower your confidence becomes, so it becomes a vicious circle. Most of the worry is effectively habitual and you become used to feeling like this. It is often irrational, too. It is important firstly to recognise the worry and then try to step back and rationalise the situation and try to put things into perspective.

It may be helpful to talk through the worry with a friend or think about what advice you would give a friend if the roles were reversed. Keep rationalising the situation and try to realise that the worry is not helping you. Try to focus on the reality and the positives of the situation. The more you do this, the less you will worry and it will become more habitual not to feel so anxious, nervous and scared. More often than not, people with low confidence begin to develop irrational fears, so it is really important that you are able to recognise these fears and mentally banish them from your mind.

'You can never cross the ocean unless you have the courage to lose sight of the shore.'

Examples of past events or situations you have feared and why you feared them?	What actually happened? Was it as bad as you thought it would be? Did your worse fears come true? Did you survive?
e.g. I had to go to a friend's wedding on my own and was so scared of being on my own and having nobody to talk to	It was ok! Actually it was better than ok. Everyone was really friendly and there were other people there on their own and I made some new friends.

CHAPTER 3 SUMMARY

The Chimp Paradox is an excellent book and model to understand, and can be extremely beneficial in understanding your thoughts and behaviours and how it is possible to control these in a way that is much more beneficial to you and your life. Keep looking to recognise on a daily basis the difference between Chimp and Human mode, and practise the techniques to manage and reassure the Chimp. It is also vital that you realise how many positive things there are in your life and how you can deal with negative situations that arise.

You are much stronger and resilient than you realise – and you will become even stronger going forward – so keep going.

Chapter 4

Triggers, Assumptions & Self-Help

Objectives:

We start to look at how you can really help yourself to overcome anxiety with a range of self-help recommendations, and also look at some of the common triggers and anxiety-provoking assumptions.

Self-help recommendations

My personal view is that the best way to deal with and overcome issues of the mind – like stress, anxiety, and depression

is to understand yourself as much as possible and then understand what tools, techniques, and other methods or treatments are best for you to focus on and use to manage any issues. You are the best person to help yourself, but that will be greatly improved if you know yourself and what will work best for you.

By helping yourself you are in control, and being in control is a very powerful and effective place to be. You can decide when, what, how, how much, etc. rather than relying on other people or other things that may not be reliable or as effective or available when needed. Of course, outside help, support and advice can be very useful and should be used but ultimately it is your life and your issues and they are best dealt with by you.

There is no magic wand to instantly cure everything. It will take time, effort, patience and commitment on your part, but the results will be worth it. Being in control, having the understanding, knowing yourself and what will work for you is where you want to be and you can get there.

In this section I look at general areas to think about, consider and to work on that you can do yourself and developing self-help techniques. Most of these will apply and be effective if you take time to think about them and put them into practice and then keep practising. The more you practise, the easier it will become.

Control

One of the main causes and characteristics of anxiety is not feeling in control. When you are in control and feel that you have things under control then you are more confident, more secure, more rational, less anxious, more relaxed, and generally in a better place. However, in so many situations, particularly when anxiety is present, we must understand that many things are out of our control and there is nothing we can do about it. You can't control what you can't control, but you can control how you respond to it.

Ask yourself whether or not you can change anything or have any control over other people or events. Often the answer is no. You then have to accept this and let it go. Stop thinking, stop analysing, stop trying to control or influence, and accept you cannot do anything. The best thing you can do is to think about something else, which is under your control, and that will be positive and productive for you.

An example of this is feeling like you are waiting for a relationship. If that is what you feel you want from life, then you accept that you cannot directly affect this; it is one of the things that will happen when it happens. To feel more in control, think about how you can develop yourself in ways that will make you feel more valuable in that relationship when it comes; learn to cook, learn to drive, develop your DIY skills, climb a mountain, and get a sense of achievement in your own right. Remember that you want a relationship, you don't need it, and when it comes you can say this is what I am bringing to the table; you are valuable, and you and your partner can go on to enhance each other's lives, not one being dependent on the other.

'If you don't like something, change it; if you can't change it, change the way you think about it.'

Worry and Overthinking

Nearly all of us are guilty of worrying too much and overthinking at times and for some people, particularly those with anxiety issues, worrying and overthinking are a major part of life. However, it is not helpful or beneficial and causes so much unnecessary and increased stress, pressure and anxiety that lead to further problems.

The best advice on this is to read through the following quotes, again and again. Keep reminding yourself that worry is not productive, not helpful, not beneficial, and is a waste of time. Whenever you feel yourself worrying and overthinking something tell yourself to stop, and keep practising this. It becomes easier. Just like worrying becomes a habit, you can make it a good habit to not worry and overthink. You could use Post-it notes to write down the quotes and put them in places you will see them for easy reference. Or if you find you overthink mostly at night, then tell one to yourself before you go to bed.

'Worrying doesn't take away tomorrow's troubles, it takes away today's peace.'

'Most of the things you worry about never happen.'

'A day of worry is more exhausting than a week of work.'

'Worrying will never change the outcome.'

'Remember, today is the tomorrow you worried about yesterday.'

'Overthinking – the art of creating problems that weren't even there.'

'90% of our problems are caused by our own thoughts.'

'Overthinking kills your happiness.'

'I think too much and then put myself in a bad mood.'

'Overthinking only complicates your life and causes stress.'

'Overthinking ruins you. Ruins the situation, twists things around, makes you worry and just makes everything much worse than it actually is.'

'Don't believe everything you think!'

'Worrying is like a rocking chair, it gives you something to do but doesn't get you anywhere.'

Best friend advice and being your own best friend

One of the most effective and helpful bits of advice I can offer in any situation is to think about what you would say to your best friend or someone you really cared about if they came to you with exactly the same issues and problems you are facing. With the information, knowledge and understanding of the situation what would you say to them to offer the best advice for their best interests?

This is a powerful and effective method of dealing with your own problems, issues and anxieties, as you are more likely to be rational, unbiased, less emotional, and more reasoned in your attempts to help. So do this and apply it to yourself. Too often we can get too caught up in our own thoughts and we can be too harsh on ourselves. So by thinking about the same situation, but from a different perspective, it can really help. Take the same advice that you would give your best friend.

Something else that is really important, yet so many of us don't do this, is to be your own best friend! Be nice to yourself, look out for yourself, care about yourself, do the right things for yourself, be there for yourself and generally treat yourself like you would treat your best friend.

It is of course very important and beneficial to have people in your life who care for you, love you, respect you, and support you. However, the most important person in your life is you. You are the only person who will always be there 100% of the time, so if you can treat yourself well and be your own best friend then that will be incredibly beneficial for you. It is not being selfish; it is simply a case of doing what is right for you, and that will have a positive impact on everyone else that you care about and who is important in your life. So be your own best friend.

Here are some example situations of someone with high anxiety	If this was your best friend asking you for help and advice in each example what would you say to them?
I have had some blood tests and a scan for breast cancer and the results aren't due for 7 days – I am so worried and so scared.	
I am going on holiday to Mexico which I'm sure will be great but I hate flying and I am so scared. I'm not sleeping as a result and would prefer not to go at all.	
I've entered a 10km charity running event which is only a few weeks away and I don't feel I can do it. I hurt my ankle and I have not trained as much as I should have done and I'm so worried about the race and letting everyone down.	
I'm so stressed with work and I'm so worried about an upcoming review and appraisal. I don't get on with my boss and what they demand is impossible. What if I lose my job?	
My daughter is going to be starting university in a few months and I'm so worried about how she will cope being away from home. She's going to be at least 3 hours away so what will I do if she needs my help?	
I've booked a weekend away with my partner for our anniversary in London, including a concert, but I hate crowds and I'm terrified of the underground and hate how busy London is. I'm really not looking forward to this and would rather just stay at home.	

Questions to ask yourself

When feeling anxious and worrying it is very easy to get so preoccupied in the negative thought-process, overthink and make the situation worse. A good practical suggestion is to step back for a few moments and ask yourself a few straightforward questions. These are designed to make you think more clearly and give some perspective. Spend some time thinking about your answers and ensure you are really honest with yourself.

Example questions to ask yourself:

- How important is this really?
- In a year from now will it really matter?
- Have I dealt with this or similar situations before?
- Is what I am doing or thinking actually productive and helping me?
- Can I actually change anything here?
- Do I have all the facts?
- Am I thinking rationally?

Negative thinking

It can be very easy to think about worst-case scenarios or generally think negatively about situations, events, circumstances, and people when you are feeling anxious – much more so than would be considered normal. You can effectively become paranoid and if not addressed quickly and effectively, this can become very dangerous.

Often we will not have all the facts regarding a situation and the more anxious we are, the more likely we are to fill the 'facts gap' with negative or paranoid thinking, focusing on worst-case outcomes, views, actions, etc. For example, if we are particularly anxious about a relationship and then don't hear back from a partner, say from a text message, we might start imagining all kinds of negative possibilities (far more than any normal or positive possibilities) such as being involved in an accident or them cheating on you.

Occasionally our paranoid, negative, worst-case thoughts may be right. There is perhaps a very small possibility that we are correct and if in the past you have been proved correct on an occasion then you will be more likely to be more paranoid and think of more negative outcomes. However, this is still very unlikely and you have to 'play the odds' and get perspective. There is likely to be a normal explanation and the worry, angst, and paranoia have only caused you grief, stress and unwelcome thoughts that impact on your health and wellbeing.

Negative thinking can be very contagious as well as unproductive, unhelpful, and damaging. You have to try to stop it by either not thinking about it at all, or thinking about positive thoughts and possibilities and get a rational perspective. This is most likely achieved through practice and effort. But also consider:

- Talking to trusted friends
- Writing stuff down
- Thinking about past situations when your paranoia has been wrong
- Reminding yourself that negative thinking is not helping you
- Doing as many productive, positive, beneficial things for yourself as possible.

'Stop being afraid and thinking about what could go wrong and instead focus on what could go right.'

Physical activity and exercise

We all know that exercise and being active are good for us, though most people associate this with physical health benefits. However, physical activity has huge benefits to our emotional and mental health, too, including being very effective at reducing anxiety. There are direct benefits to the brain in terms of reducing stress, improving mood, and regulating neurotransmitters. In addition there are indirect benefits of feeling in better shape, increased confidence, and a sense of pride and achievement in doing the exercise. All of which has a positive impact on any anxiety issues.

Any form of activity is good for you and if you are able to do any group activities or team events with a friend then the social interaction can be an added benefit. Think about what you currently do and what more you could do. Going to a gym, attending classes, joining a running club, having a game of tennis, going on a hike, or climbing a mountain, for example, are all great ways of being healthy and at the same time helping with any anxiety issues. You can also look to do exercise at home or at work – basically any extra physical activity you can do will have a positive effect on you and can help you overcome the anxiety.

Write down a list of physical activities and exercise you can start doing, and go and make the effort to do them!

e.g. I will join a local running club, I will start swimming again, I will re-join the yoga classes I used to go to

Triggers and Anxiety-provoking assumptions

Anxiety-provoking assumptions (APAs) are assumptions or triggers that can cause or magnify anxious feelings and behaviours. People have many different APAs and they will vary considerably from individual to individual, but here are five of the most common ones:

Perfectionism – Perfectionists often assume they must do everything right or they will have failed totally and the consequences will be devastating. They worry over small details and blow things out of proportion with their expectations. If you are a perfectionist you will be very self-critical and unlikely to see any positives if you feel you have failed.

Vulnerability – If you have this type of APA, you may constantly worry about possible disasters and things that could go wrong. You may feel at the mercy of life's forces and as such live your life feeling vulnerable and on edge. You will imagine worst-case scenarios like losing your job, then your house and car, then your partner, etc.

Control – If you have the control assumption, you always want to be in control and be the driver, rather than the passenger. This is because they feel you can't trust other people or rely on anyone other than yourself. You will focus on why other people can't do things right and assume this then causes all the issues.

Approval – People with this assume they require the approval of others for anything and everything, and that can be at any cost to themselves. They hate and can't stand any form of criticism, and are always seeking approval. You will worry about whether your boss likes you, for example.

Dependency – In this case it is those people who feel they can't survive on their own and are dependent upon others. They need other people in their lives all the time and turn to others for help. You will look to others for support and approval, even though you may have the solutions to any problems yourself.

We all make assumptions all the time and these can be important, helpful and necessary in our lives. However, some deep-rooted assumptions we have can cause issues and as we can see above they can trigger anxiety. Take time to think about your own APAs and possible triggers that occur in your life that can impact on your anxiety. Be honest and try to identify your assumptions so you are more aware of yourself in this respect.

The next stage is to try to break down these assumptions as much as you can. Challenge yourself and the assumptions so that they become less of a factor. It is much better to base things on facts, evidence and reality, rather than assumptions. Try to understand why you may have had those assumptions and where they have come from. The more you are aware of any assumptions and the more you can then reduce or eliminate them, the better it will be for you.

Write down some examples of anxiety-provoking assumptions you have had	What type of assumptions were they and were your assumptions fully correct?
e.g. my son is climbing Mount Snowdon for part of his Duke of Edinburgh Award and I've heard it can be really dangerous and the weather forecast looks awful. What if he falls and breaks his leg or he gets lost and is left stranded on the mountain? He's my only son and I couldn't bear it if anything bad happens to him.	This is mainly 'Vulnerability' with some aspect of 'Control' assumptions. Vulnerable in the sense of focusing on the worst-case scenarios and expecting terrible things to happen. Control in the sense of not being there and having to leave it in the hands of others – in this case well-trained, experienced, qualified leaders.

Travel light

Most of us are guilty of carrying excess baggage or hoarding, in both a physical sense and a mental and emotional way. You are likely to have loads of stuff in your house that you don't need, taking up space and cluttering your home, which is unnecessary and unhelpful to you. The same applies to your mind.

If you can release this excess baggage, let things go and travel lighter you will feel more free and less burdened. You will be able to do more, have more room for other things if needed, and generally feel lighter. Focus on carrying just your own stuff and don't be weighed down and burdened by other people's baggage. Think of life as a long journey – it will be easier and you will be able to do more if you travel light!

It is easier said than done but if you make a concerted effort to reduce your load, free yourself up, let things go that are no longer helpful to you, then it will make a big difference to your life. Don't be weighed down by baggage you pick up on your way. You don't need it and your life is likely to be much better without it, so make those changes and travel light.

'Sometimes you don't realise the weight of something you've been carrying until you feel the weight of its release.'

When are you not anxious?

Take a bit of time to think about the times when you are not anxious and feel more comfortable and relaxed. There will be reasons and explanations for this so try to understand these reasons. What times, situations, circumstances, people, events, etc. make you feel relaxed and not anxious? Think about why these factors make you less anxious and see how you can learn from this to help manage and prevent your anxiety.

There are probably a whole range of factors and things you do or could do that will put you in a more relaxed place, so think carefully about how you can do more to focus on these and why these help. There is never a simple quick fix or instant miracle, but by understanding and thinking about the times you are not anxious you will be better placed to do the right things to get yourself to that place more often.

Think about when you are actively and totally engaged in something that you really enjoy doing and that comes naturally to you. It may be your job, but could be a hobby, sport or social interaction. Usually at times like these you simply don't have time to think about your anxieties.

CHAPTER 4 SUMMARY

This chapter we have started to focus on the many practical self-help recommendations that exist. Some will resonate and be more influential to you than others, but there are so many areas to consider and so much you can do to help yourself. A lot of the time you know the answers already and know what will be best for you – but it's a case of reminding yourself, convincing yourself and believing in yourself. By completing the exercises and asking yourself the questions, you will allow yourself the time to make better choices to reduce and manage the anxiety. well done on reaching the halfway mark. Keep using the tools and practising the techniques you are developing – it will become easier the more you do.

HALFWAY

How are you getting on?

You should be noticing some improvements with the knowledge you are gaining and from working on some of the techniques and utilising your tools. Remember that you will undoubtedly have some bad days during this whole process, but the key is that overall you are on the up, and building momentum. Take some time to reflect on what you have achieved so far and write down below some of the positives from the last few chapters.

What's working?	Why is it working?
e.g. I've become very good at recognising when I am in Chimp mode	e.g. By recognising being in Chimp mode it allows me to then step back and see how I can get the Human to take control – usually it's a simple case of reassuring the Chimp that everything will be ok and I'll look after him. Everything is then much calmer and I feel more in control.

Chapter 5
More Self-Help & Instant Tips

Objectives:

We continue with the self-help recommendations this chapter, including the relationship between sleep and anxiety, and also included are a few practical instant help tips to try out.

Sleep and Anxiety

The most common reason for poor sleep is anxiety, worrying, and over-thinking at night-time. So it is likely that you will often suffer from poor sleep, which then has additional negative knock-on effects and can include increased anxiety. It can become a vicious circle of anxiety, causing poor sleep, and the tiredness can result in increased anxiety, and so on. So it is really important to focus on your sleep and this should improve with you overcoming the anxiety issues. However, it is worth reading through the following areas relating to sleep to see if you can make your own improvements in this respect.

'I want to sleep but my brain won't stop talking to itself!'

Invest in better sleep

Ideally we would be spending nearly one-third of our entire lives asleep, and we know that sleep is extremely important to our health and happiness. It has such an influence on our lives, for better or worse, so it makes sense that we should invest in better sleep. If sleep is a problem then take some time to consider how important it is to you and what effect it has on your life. Then consider what you can do in terms of investing in better sleep, which could be financial investment or time investment or both. As an example, you could buy a new bed or mattress which could be a lot of money but actually if it meant a difference to your quality of sleep over many months, or indeed years, it is likely to be money very well spent. There will always be things you can do that could make a difference to your quality of sleep, and although they may involve a cost or your time, make sure you think clearly about all the benefits that could occur as a result, and rather than seeing things as a cost look at them as an investment in your health and happiness.

'Sleep is the best meditation' – the Dalai Lama

Stop struggling

If you have sleep problems, whether they are long-term or temporary, then it is likely that it plays on your mind for much of the time. So, in addition to all the consequences of poor sleep both physically and mentally, there may be other downsides. During the day you may well be thinking about your lack of sleep and be anxious about whether you will sleep that night or be looking back on your previous poor night's sleep. This additional anxiety is then counterproductive.

As much as you can, stop struggling! Stop thinking about your sleep problems. Stop focusing on the negative aspects and concerns around the problem. Accept you can't change anything about the past and worrying about the next night won't help. And if you are lying in bed unable to get to sleep, or you wake up during the night and then can't sleep, try your best not to focus on that. The more you struggle, the worse it will be. Accepting the situation and then focusing on what you can do in the way of potential solutions will be more beneficial. If you find yourself lying in bed unable to sleep, rather than focusing on the fact you can't sleep, try the tactic of accepting it and stop struggling. Try to focus on what might work in a productive way and relax. That is far more likely to work than struggling and getting more wound up by the situation.

'Man should forget his anger before he lies down to sleep.' – Gandhi

CBT

Cognitive behavioural therapy (CBT) is a relatively new therapy, but is becoming increasingly popular and effective in helping people with a variety of issues linked to their thoughts, feelings, and behaviours, and can thus also help with sleep. It is really about finding techniques that work to correct a person's negative way of thinking and correcting self-destructive and damaging behaviour. Issues such as phobias, obsessions, stress, anxiety, depression, eating disorders, substance abuse, addictions, and sleeping problems can all be helped with effective CBT. In fact, in recent years, CBT has proved the most effective treatment for insomnia.

A lot of sleep problems are an effect of other issues that CBT can help with as people change their thinking and behaviour and understand more about their negative habitual thought processes so that they develop more positive and beneficial behaviours. You can 'unlearn' the negative thoughts and replace them with much more productive, positive thoughts.

Relax/wind down

Modern life can be very hectic, busy and stressful, and many of us will struggle with being able to relax and wind down sufficiently to then be able to sleep once we go to bed, and then sleep well. You cannot expect to be able to be asleep straightaway if you are still buzzing, excited, anxious, stressed, etc. and have not relaxed or wound down enough.

So try to ensure, as you approach the time you would typically go to sleep, that you are doing things that will help you to relax. Try to take your mind off any worries, stresses, or issues of the day. Try not to overthink too much or concern yourself with things that you cannot do anything about right now. Perhaps watch some TV or a film, read a book or magazine, or have a nice, warm bath. The more relaxed you are, the greater the chances of you sleeping once you go to bed, and once in bed either continue to wind down further, perhaps by reading or listening to some relaxing music, or try to switch off and sleep straight away.

Specific sleep exercises

Relaxation and breathing – Stressful lifestyles, working late, and watching intense television shows or the news, are some of the factors that can contribute to the mind racing and being unable to wind down. It's important to know the importance of being relaxed before bed, and to have the knowledge of effective relaxation techniques to apply in order to experience deep, restful sleep.

Relax your body – This can be done in bed and works by relaxing separate groups of muscles. It is also effective to visualise each set of muscles being relaxed as you go through the exercise:

- Tense a muscle by contracting and flexing for 7–10 seconds.
- Don't strain the muscle.
- Visualise the muscle being tensed and feel the build-up of tension.
- Release each muscle abruptly, then relax, allowing the body to go limp before going on to the next muscle.
- Keep other muscles relaxed whilst working on a particular muscle.

Breathe – The effects of deep breathing are largely psychological but it can bring about a very positive physiological response in the body. It can normalise the heart and respiration rate and relax you, taking away some of the stresses and anxiety that you may have.

An exercise:

As well as relaxing you before bed, you can use this breathing exercise whenever anything upsetting happens, and before you react. It can be done anywhere because you don't have to lie on your back:

- Sit up with your back straight and place the tip of your tongue just behind your upper front teeth, and keep it there throughout the entire exercise.
- Practise exhaling with your tongue in this position. It will be easier if you purse your lips.
- Now close your mouth and inhale through your nose for four seconds (counting one one thousand, two one thousand, etc.).
- Hold your breath for seven seconds then exhale through your mouth, taking eight seconds to exhale completely.
- Repeat three to four times and try to be accurate with the counting.

Try to do this regularly, as the more you do, the better you will become and the greater the benefits, and if you can get into a routine of doing this every evening before bed you should see the positive effects.

Your bedroom

As far as possible, and as practical, you should ensure your bedroom is primarily about sleeping and make it as conducive to sleep for you as you can. You should associate your bedroom and your bed with sleep with as few other distractions as possible. Apart from sex, the less other things you do in bed, the better, other than sleep. Having that strong, consistent association between your bed and sleep will allow you to focus on sleep and more likely improve the quality and quantity.

If you have lots of other things going on in your bedroom which are not sleep-related then these potential distractions or associations with non-sleep activities could be a detriment to your sleeping habits. So, for example, watching TV, playing computer games, eating food, working, having work-related implements like a laptop and phone, plus in-depth conversation with your partner can all be a bad influence on your sleep.

Air quality

Ensuring that you have plenty of fresh, good-quality air in your bedroom can play an important role in your sleep. A stuffy, poorly oxygenated room is not going to help so it is helpful to open doors and windows, letting fresh air pass through when possible. There are practical issues like potential noise or the cold that can at times prevent this, but by using your initiative and planning in advance it is possible to ensure clean, fresh air does circulate through your room, aiding your breathing and sleeping.

Also, be aware of potential allergies that could come from pollen, general dust or dust mites, particularly if you have asthma or hay fever, and if necessary seek advice or do air quality tests if you think this may be a problem.

Write things down

Sometimes while we are lying in bed unable to sleep it is helpful to write things down on a notepad if certain thoughts pop into our head. Keeping a pen and pad near your bedside can be useful so that if you are worrying or thinking about issues then you can write them down and tell yourself you will come back to those in the morning. It could be you have a fantastic idea or thought, and in a similar way you are likely to be better off by writing it down and then forgetting about it so you can sleep and come back to it in the morning. Otherwise you may not be able to stop thinking about it, get excited, release some adrenaline, and your sleep will definitely be compromised.

You may wake up with a particular thought, idea, or issue and by writing it down it could help you relax again and go back to sleep. Knowing that you have documented it should mean you don't have to worry about remembering it or focusing on it whilst it would be better for you to be sleeping. You could try writing a 'worry diary' whereby you jot down your worries and concerns, which may help you to leave them on your notepad and not in your head at bedtime.

Sleep-inducing scents

There are certain smells and scents such as lavender, geranium, chamomile, and ylang-ylang that can activate the alpha wave activity in the back of your brain, which can help to relax you and therefore provide a better environment for falling asleep and aid in you sleeping more soundly.

So perhaps try mixing a few drops of these essential oils with some water in a spray bottle and use a little on your pillows and sheets. You could also try having a bowl of potpourri in your bedroom. Additionally, if you find yourself sleeping away from home in a hotel, friend's or family's house, for example, then you could take it with you and use so that it helps replicate your own normal sleep environment and thus aid your sleep.

Visualise feeling sleepy

You could try visualising stages of going to sleep whilst you are lying in bed trying to sleep. Focus on yourself and visualise how it would look and feel to be very tired, relaxed, yawning, feeling drowsy, switching off, and then falling asleep. By focusing on this and really visualising yourself doing this could actually help you fall asleep.

It will hopefully take your mind off other thoughts and help you wind down, and you can almost trick your body and mind into sleep through this visualisation.

It may not always work, or it may take practice to make it effective, but it is worth trying as you have nothing to lose and it could make a big difference. So again, go over in your head how it would look in an ideal situation where you were tired, feeling drowsy, relaxing, and drifting off to sleep in your bed, and if necessary keep repeating this visualisation technique. The more you practise, the better you will become at it and the more effective it will be.

Refocus on something else

You may go to bed with a whole mix of thoughts or perhaps something very specific which is occupying your mind and preventing you from sleeping. Although it is never as easy as it sounds, try to refocus your thoughts onto something else. Make it something relaxing, positive, or productive.

A few things I have tried with success over the years include visualising a gym workout, packing for a trip, or thinking about a spa day. So with the gym workout I will visualise the gym with the weights and machines and then go through in my head the different exercises and routines and what muscles I will be working and keep going through the wide range. I may start with some bicep curls, then some triceps dips focusing on my arms, then some sit-ups and chest presses, etc. Basically go through in my head a routine that I am familiar with until I fall asleep. This is positive, productive, familiar and relaxing, and will often work well.

Perhaps you could try visualising your favourite place or a tranquil scene such as a lake or a mountain, the sounds of a gentle stream, or a walk in the woods. Retrace your steps on a favourite walk, taking particular notice of the sounds, the scents, the colours, the feel of the earth beneath your feet and the light as it filters through the trees. Observe the wild flowers, or fungi, or the different leaves on the trees above your head. Or just fix in your mind a certain scene. A lake is always great. Note the stillness, the reflections, and the sound of absolute silence.

Solutions, not problems

If you find yourself worrying or thinking about a particular problem or several problems and you cannot switch off from it then try as much as possible to think about potential solutions to that problem rather than the problem itself. If you are not sleeping then you may as well use that time productively and focus on coming up with solutions. You should also find that by focusing on solutions this is more positive and productive and will give you more chance of relaxing and feeling less anxious, so more likely to help with sleep.

So whatever the problems, keep telling yourself to think about solutions instead. For example, it could be work issues that are occupying your mind. An important meeting or presentation coming up, too much work to do, a work colleague causing you problems, a member of your staff who is not performing, etc. Turn your thought-process to working out possible solutions like how you will prepare and plan, who should you talk to and how will you approach it, what help is there available, prioritise your time and realise you cannot do everything, set up a meeting with a mentor, etc. The more productive your thoughts, the better it will be for you, and the more you practise this, the easier it becomes.

Consult with Doctor

If you are really struggling with your sleep, particularly if it seems to be a longer-term, ongoing issue, then you should consult with your doctor for advice. There may be additional help or suggestions available. The doctor may discuss medication, may provide some helpful literature or ideas, or they could refer you to a specialist or a sleep lab for further analysis and assessment. Poor sleep is a very common problem, yet people are often reluctant to seek professional help. There may not be any miracle cures or quick fixes but there may be some helpful advice and things to take away, either to try out or to think about how they may be beneficial.

Also, it could be that your sleep problems are more a result of a different condition, illness, or health problem which could be identified by discussing with the doctor. Often there will be more specific underlying reasons for your difficulty sleeping, and if they are addressed, managed, or treated then your sleep may well improve significantly. So don't be afraid to go to your doctor as you have nothing to lose and potentially a lot to gain.

Medication

The most common and well known treatment for insomnia is sleep-inducing medication, also known as hypnotics. The most common type of hypnotic are a group of drugs called benzodiazepines, and the most well-known of these is diazepam (Valium) which is used to treat anxiety and acts as a muscle relaxant, and has been around since the early 1960s. Similar drugs, like temazepam, can be useful for short-term insomnia, but there is little evidence to suggest that they are appropriate for chronic insomnia. Also they may also cause side effects and possibly a sense of drowsiness during the day.

Another commonly used group of drugs developed more recently are the benzodiazepine receptor agonists. Sometimes these are called 'Z drugs', since many of their names begin with the letter 'Z' (zopiclone and zolpidem, for example). There are various other groups of drugs that may potentially be prescribed for insomnia; melatonin receptor agonists aim to promote sleep by increasing the amount of melatonin in the body; orexin antagonists aim to limit the hormone orexin which is related to being awake; and some antihistamines and (rarely) opioids can be used as sedatives.

Some antidepressants do have a sedative effect, and research has shown that people who were treated using a combination of sleeping medication and antidepressants showed greater improvements in depressive symptoms than people who used antidepressants only. However, the British Association for Psychopharmacology advises against using antidepressants in the treatment of insomnia as there is limited evidence indicating their efficacy in this application. It is difficult to gauge how many prescriptions are written for hypnotics because many of these drugs are prescribed for problems that are not directly sleep-related. And again, the side effects from these drugs may cause debilitation and other common physical problems.

Herbal remedies

Many different varieties of natural sleep remedies are available and promoted as sleep aids with mixed evidence as to their effectiveness. However, some have been shown to work and they are certainly worth exploring as long as you have done some research and are careful. Many chemists and other health shops will sell a range of herbal sleep aid products, but please read the labels and if possible discuss them with a pharmacist for additional advice.

Examples of herbal sleep aids include melatonin, valerian root, and chamomile, and can come in different formats like tablets or tea bags. Be aware that they can potentially cause some side effects such as headaches and stomach upsets. However, as with most things, people react and respond differently and it is certainly worth trying a wide variety of things that could be beneficial and work out for yourself if it works or not, and speak to friends and colleagues to see if they have tried any herbal remedies and what were their experiences.

Beds, mattresses, duvets, and sheets

It should go without saying that the right bed for you will make a difference to your sleep quality and quantity. Whether that's the right size, a firm or soft mattress, or a special supporting one, it is worth finding out as best you can what is the best bed for you and invest in it. Of course, the sheets, blankets, and duvet are also important, and again think about investing in these for your long-term health and happiness rather than just a one-off expense. Also change and wash your sheets and covers often and think about your bed and bedding as vital not only for sleep, but also your overall wellbeing.

A great example of the importance of having the right mattress, sheets, duvet, etc., so that you sleep as well as possible, is what Team Sky do for their cyclists. (Team Sky are the British-based professional cycling team, who have had major success with the likes of Sir Bradley Wiggins and Chris Froome winning the Tour de France.) They have a general philosophy called 'marginal gains' which is effectively saying that there are literally hundreds of factors that contribute or effect the performance of the team, and if they can improve all of these even by very small 'marginal gains' then the cumulative effect will become significant and make a real difference.

So when it comes to sleep, Team Sky ensure that they take their own pillows, sheets, mattresses, and duvets with them throughout the different tours and numerous different hotels. This means the cyclists have consistency each night and are much more likely to sleep better, which is a very important ingredient in helping them perform at their best.

Temperature

I'm sure everyone has experienced at some point that horrible feeling of being so hot at night that you just can't sleep no matter what you do. No duvet, no covers, no sheets, no clothes, windows open, fans on, etc., yet still it is too hot and uncomfortable to sleep. Conversely you may have had those nights where you are so cold that you are curled up and shivering and unable to sleep. The latter example tends to be less common due to heating and decent duvets etc., but the former problem can be more common as people tend not to have air conditioning at home.

Your body temperature plays a key role in how well you sleep, and your body temperature changes at different stages of sleep. Typically you need to be cool in order to provide the best environment to sleep, and although everyone is slightly different you should consider how you can have the optimum temperature for you.

Apart from opening windows, having fans (stand-up and ceiling), using air conditioning, lighter-tog duvets, fewer blankets, fewer clothes on, etc. think about other things you can try that could help. That could include on very hot nights sleeping in a separate bed to your partner so you are both more likely to sleep better. Or a cool bath/shower prior to sleep to reduce body temperature could be beneficial.

Light

Light is vitally important to our sleep cycles and can, for many people, play a major role in their sleep, both negatively and positively. In general terms, when you are asleep your surroundings should be dark with no light at all. So ensuring that no artificial lights are on and no natural light can get through from windows or doors is necessary.

Many people have experienced a bedroom light being switched on during the night which wakes you up and then it is often hard to get back to sleep, or if a bright ray of sunshine peeks through your curtains and wakes you. Your brain will naturally react by suppressing the release of melatonin and prepare itself to be awake and alert. So to prevent your brain and body waking up prematurely due to light make sure you do all you can to mitigate the risk, which can include wearing an eye mask, using blackout blinds, time-sensitive artificial lights, etc. And ensure the light bulbs in your room are not too bright, or even better, are on a dimmer switch.

Conversely, though, light can be helpful in ensuring you don't sleep for too long, and there is a danger that if all light is cut out and then you wake up from your alarm, you will feel groggy. So many people like to use artificial wake-up lights that slowly get brighter over many minutes before an alarm is set off. This prepares the brain, signalling that wake-up time is approaching and people will often feel much more alert and awake when they open their eyes.

Exercise and be active

Being more physically active and doing more exercise is very likely to help you sleep better. So apart from all the other fantastic benefits of exercise, the fact that it is a proven way to improve your sleep should be a good motivator to do more. There are several direct reasons why exercise helps people to sleep better, as well as several indirect reasons.

The human body is designed to exercise regularly and has evolved on the basis of being very physically active, so it makes sense that the natural cycle includes activity during the day and rest (sleep) at night. This basic concept has served humans well for many hundreds of thousands of years. So if we don't exercise and are not physically active it makes sense that our sleep could be affected. There is that common saying that after a hard day of physical exertion 'you will sleep well tonight'. And this is generally true.

Be careful not to exercise vigorously too late in the day and close to bedtime, as the various positive chemicals and hormones released as a result of exercise will make you more alert and energised for a while and it may be more difficult to wind down ready for sleep. So be sensible in what you do and when you do it, but be assured, exercise and physical activity will help you to improve your quality of sleep.

'A well-spent day brings happy sleep.'
Leonardo da Vinci

The last hour

What you do during the last hour leading up to you going to sleep, or trying to go to sleep, can play a vital role in your sleep success. Ideally during the last hour you will be relaxing and winding down and effectively preparing for a good night's sleep. Factors such as not eating or drinking, not exercising, not watching anything too stimulating (like a horror film!), not exposing yourself to bright lights, not working or thinking about difficult issues that may play on your mind, and of course going to the toilet can all help towards a better sleep.

Having a constructive bedtime routine can also help, as well as trying to go to bed at the same time each night and avoid any stimulants such as nicotine and caffeine. Try to switch off phones, computers, electrical devices, and anything else that may stimulate the brain or affect your eyes.

Sleep positions

Have you ever thought much about your own sleeping position? Do you have a favourite or one you find yourself getting into naturally? For most people they have what they would call their normal sleeping position and the most common is the foetal position, replicating how a baby in the womb tends to position itself. There are three main sleeping positions with variables of each: side, back, and stomach. Sleep specialists recommend sleeping on your side in order to rest more comfortably and decrease the likelihood of interrupted sleep. While there are many variations of sleeping on your side, all of which are beneficial in helping to alleviate insomnia and chronic sleep deprivation, the most comfortable position involves bending the knees slightly upwards towards the chest area.

Snooze button

Take the snooze button challenge which is to force yourself to get up as soon as the alarm goes off and never use the snooze button again (ok, maybe on a special occasion!). You will find once you are in the habit of waking up as soon as your alarm goes off you can set it to a later time and you are more likely to get a longer, deeper, more effective sleep.

Making assumptions and judgements

We spend much of our time making assumptions and judgements about events and people, and much of this is necessary and natural. But we often make unfair and incorrect assumptions and judgements, which can cause issues both to ourselves and to other people. You have heard the expression, 'don't judge a book by its cover' and you will be aware that you shouldn't make judgements without having all the facts or hearing both sides to the story, but that doesn't seem to stop us. Also, when we are going through our own difficult times it seems that we tend to make even more unhelpful, damaging, and potentially destructive assumptions and judgements.

Making negative assumptions and judgements about events and people is increased and connected to being more paranoid and insecure, and having lower self-esteem. This in turn causes more paranoia, suspicion and concern that further lower self-esteem and makes us think up even more negative and unhelpful assumptions and judgements. It is a vicious circle and difficult to get out of, unless you recognise what you may be doing and act upon that.

Try not to make assumptions or judgements unless you are confident you have all the facts and a full understanding. The chances are you don't. Try to find out more or don't think or worry about it at all. Do not feed your paranoia with negative possibilities and focus on unhelpful and unproductive scenarios. Instead, try focusing on things that will increase your self-esteem and reduce the paranoid thoughts, and have a much more open mind. You might not be able to control what other people do and think, but you do have a choice over what you do and think.

Spin bike class example

I often go to a spin class at the gym where there is a room full of stationary bikes with digital displays that show measurements like RPM, watts, time, calories, gear setting, and distance. There are often thirty or more participants in the class and I think this is a great example, or analogy, of how easy it is to make assumptions based on very little knowledge.

Imagine you go into the class and briefly, for a minute or so, observe a few people with the aim of determining who is the best or fittest. You will make initial judgements and assumptions based upon appearance, their physique, what they are wearing, their age, etc. You then look at the digital display briefly on their bikes and make further assumptions before making your conclusions. You have a lot of evidence and knowledge to make an informed conclusion. However, think about all the other factors that you will not know about which are likely to substantially influence your findings if you knew. For example:

- They may not be feeling well that day
- They may have a big event or race coming up so just taking it easy
- They may have just done a big event or race so doing a slower, easier recovery ride

- The bikes are not all calibrated equally so results will vary depending on what bike is used
- They may temporarily be taking a break or taking it easy during the class
- They may be recovering from illness or injury
- It may be their second consecutive class

There are probably several other factors that are relevant but not taken into account. So the point here is that you may think you have lots of knowledge or evidence but the fact is there is usually so much more that you don't know and therefore any conclusions made can be weak, fragile, or plain wrong.

So be careful when making your judgements and assumptions about people and situations, as it is more than likely you do not have all the facts and knowledge and making such conclusions can potentially be harmful, unfair, hurtful, and damaging to all those concerned, including yourself.

Jealousy and Comparisons

It is very easy to become jealous of someone and be envious of someone else's position or their particular circumstances. They have this or that, they look like that, they have money, they have the job, they have the car, they have the house, they have the partner, etc. – a never-ending list of how someone else has it better than you. Now if that list was genuine and then you were able to use it in a motivational, aspirational, inspirational, positive way, then being jealous might have some benefits.

In reality, it is much more likely that nothing positive will result from envy and jealousy. It will make you bitter, angry, upset, and negative. You will be looking for excuses and reasons and blaming others if you don't have those things you want. You will become resentful and make false assumptions and poor judgements based upon envious and subjective emotions. Envy has damaging and longer-term effects. It can eat you up, making you a jealous, bitter, and negative person who will naturally dislike people, seek to blame others, and feel the whole world is against you.

Life might not be fair, and you may have some bad luck and others some good luck, but envy and jealousy are very negative emotions. Nothing good can come of them and the sooner you get these damaging, destructive emotions out of your life, the better. If possible, whenever you feel yourself getting jealous, try to let that emotion go. Remind yourself that it is of no benefit to be feeling like that and having those thoughts. It is negative, unproductive, and potentially harmful. You don't have to be pleased for them or have any emotion towards them, just ensure that you don't have any negative, jealous thoughts, yourself, that will affect you. Just let it go.

Once you have learned how to let it go, you can take control of this harmful, negative emotion that is jealousy. It will no longer control you and damage you. You can rise above it and move forward with your life in a more positive way. Being in control of this allows you to turn other people's perceived good fortune and success into a more positive outlook for yourself.

Ask yourself why you perceive them to be fortunate and successful. Digging deeper into this area allows you to understand what you perceive success to be and allows you to think about what you want and what your aspirations might be. It may provide some goals, targets, and ambitions and you can use this as motivation to start achieving some of these. However, along that journey you may also find that a lot of the things you were previously jealous about are not actually that important after all, and your perception of fortune and success is different in reality.

As well as being envious and jealous of others we often create issues or make issues worse by comparing ourselves with other people, particularly people we know, whether that is family, friends, work colleagues, or our peers. Many people spend much of their time comparing themselves to others, which is generally a very unproductive and negative thing to do. Only if the comparisons can help you focus, work harder, and inspire and motivate you to better things can it be beneficial. Usually, though, comparisons are made in a negative way.

Firstly, everybody is different and in so many ways; therefore you will never be able to compare like for like. Secondly, you are very unlikely to ever have all the facts and information, so comparisons are always built upon assumptions and judgements and we have previously mentioned the issues with that. Thirdly, comparisons nearly always make you focus on the things you don't have as opposed to the things you do have.

People have different abilities, talents and capabilities, all with varying strengths and weaknesses and mixed with different circumstances, timing, and luck, so you just have to accept that like-for-like comparisons are not possible.

Just because someone, in your opinion, has a better car than you, or is better-looking, or has more friends, more money, a bigger house, is smarter, is healthier, is more confident, or has more luck etc., this means nothing. It is your perception and your opinion and you do not know all the facts involved, and so what anyway? Focusing on those sorts of comparisons is damaging and is much more likely to reinforce negative attitudes and beliefs and be unproductive than do anything positive for you. Try comparing less and focus more on what you have and the positive elements in your life, rather than thinking or worrying about what other people have or don't have.

Social interaction

Many people with anxiety issues tend to become more reclusive and shy away from social activities or events if they can. They don't like the feelings, the apprehension, the worry, and the stress that many social situations bring, and so would rather avoid them if possible. In some ways it can be beneficial to avoid these situations in order to reduce the anxiety and not make things worse. However, avoidance can be harmful and a careful balance needs to be adopted between managing the anxiety and making sure you don't become reclusive and lose the social interaction that is really important.

Humans need social interaction as we are very much social creatures. The more we avoid and become reclusive, the more difficult it is to regain the social interaction. Although there are times when it is likely to be advantageous to avoid people and keep yourself to yourself, generally it will be really beneficial and helpful for you to remain socially interactive and increase this social behaviour.

If you find yourself in a position where you avoid social situations and are either effectively a recluse or going that way then my advice would be to really make an effort to change this and do things that will help you be more comfortable with social interaction. If possible speak to a close friend or family member and explain your situation and ask if they will accompany you. Gradually build up the level of interaction with more people about, more talking, more engagement and interaction.

If you do find yourself with bad social anxiety and are effectively a prisoner in your own house, a first step might be to get outside your house and go for a walk on your own for a short while. Next time you may make the effort to say a 'hello' to someone you pass on your walk. You may then go to a busier area like a shopping centre where there are many people about but you don't have to engage with them. The next step may be to have a short conversation with a cashier or assistant at a shop by asking them a question or wishing them a pleasant day.

Gradually you are building up your contact with other people step by step and gaining confidence in social situations. You may try to meet up with a friend for a coffee and chat and aim to make more conversations with people, whether that's at work, at the shops or with other friends. Over time you will develop improved social skills and the confidence so that you are more comfortable and at ease in those situations and less anxious.

Build confidence

Many people lack confidence and this is often at the root of many issues, especially related to anxiety. A great way to reduce and manage anxiety is to work on understanding and building up your confidence. Another book in the series called *Boost Confidence* is recommended.

It is really important to understand what confidence is and for yourself what areas you can improve and what areas you are confident in. There are so many ways to build and develop your confidence, which will then bring so many benefits to your life and improve your health and happiness.

A particularly good way of building confidence is by doing and achieving things. Getting motivated, setting challenges for yourself and then achieving these will boost your confidence, help you face your fears and reduce your anxiety. It might not be easy but you will definitely see results and feel so much better if you give it a go, make some effort, take your time, and commit to it. You can do this!

Facing your fears

Many of our negative thoughts, behaviours, and actions are driven by fear in various ways, which can cause many additional issues. There are sometimes understandable reasons to be fearful, and often they are based upon past negative experiences in our lives. And occasionally fear can be a good thing as it can make us more alert and more focused, and prevent us from getting into danger. However, fear can be debilitating, causing additional worry, stress, and anxiety, preventing us from increasing our confidence and stopping us from doing things that will be good for us, make us happy, and improve our physical and mental health.

We are also guilty of procrastinating and putting things off, often due to fear of the outcome – fear of failure, rejection, of being laughed at, not believing it can be done, or the fear of the unknown. In most cases the best advice and the best thing for you is to just do it! There is the well-known book called *Feel the Fear and Do It Anyway*, and I would recommend that attitude.

What is the worst that could happen? Could you handle that? Have you handled similar things in the past? The answer is probably that you have, you have dealt with it, you have got through it, you have learned from it and you can do it again... if that happens. However, it might not happen and the outcome could be great! You could benefit, feel happier, feel more confident, less anxious, and more likely to embrace more stuff that will be good for you, rather than being put off or even paralysed by fear.

So stop procrastinating, step out of your comfort zone, face your fears, feel the fear and do it. In nearly all cases you will be glad you did. Remember it is better to regret the things you did than to regret the things you didn't do.

Instant help tips

There are many potential things you can do to instantly help a situation if you are feeling particularly anxious, or if you feel anxiety and stress levels building rapidly. Try as many different things as you can to see what does or doesn't work for you in any given circumstance. Here are a few ideas of instant help:

Elastic band on your wrist – Using some kind of elastic wristband, which you can pull back and release, causing a small and very quick amount of discomfort, may work. If you are feeling very anxious and thoughts are building then this technique of a short, sharp shock can effectively snap you out of those negative, unhelpful thoughts and reduce the anxiety. It is a reminder that you need to get back in control of the situation, be rational and regain perspective.

Rub the ball of your thumb – Another tip that may help is to rub or push hard in an upward movement on the ball of your thumb. The idea is that it helps reduce tension and gives you a focus to take your mind off any anxious thoughts. So both physically and mentally it can have a positive effect and can also help to get rid of headaches and general tension.

Chew gum – Another easy-to-do method of reducing anxiety and stress is to chew gum for a few minutes. Much better than biting your nails or chewing on your fingers, the act of chewing gum can be an effective and quick way of helping to reduce the tension and apprehension that might exist.

Do some vigorous exercise – Getting the heart pumping and the blood flowing plus a bit of sweat can be a very effective way of reducing anxiety in both the immediate situation and the longer term. Exercise will release endorphins and increase serotonin, helping you to feel good and forget the worry. You can focus on the positive physical activity taking your mind off the stress and anxiety, plus it will build confidence. So a quick dance, run, gym session, game of squash or some star jumps and press-ups at home can work wonders.

Finger and thumb – Squeezing the tip of a finger and your thumb together hard and at the same time thinking about a certain person you admire and respect can help boost confidence as well as reduce tension and anxiety. Think of someone who is an inspiration to you, whether that's someone you know personally or a famous sports star, actor, musician, leader, etc. By focusing for a few seconds on this person in a positive, inspiring, happy way it can take your focus away from the negative, anxious, stressful situation and give yourself an instant boost.

Breathing – There are many breathing exercises that can be effective in reducing anxiety and helping to regain control of a situation. The most simple is to make a real effort to take three really deep breaths. Another is to simply try to hold your breath for as long as possible, and a further one is to count from one to five as you breathe in and from five back down to one as you breathe out and repeat a few times. You are trying either to relax as much as possible or to take your focus away from the anxiety and on to something different, in this case breathing or holding your breath.

Music – If practical, listening to a piece of music or favourite song can be very effective in instantly reducing tension and anxiety. If you have an iPod or radio, or any kind of device that allows you to listen to music, then have it with you as much as possible and use it when it could be useful. Many people use music to help with stress, tension and anxiety and to help them relax.

Use your Senses – If you are feeling like the world is moving without you and don't feel in control, take a minute to sit and ask yourself: what can you see? What can you smell? What can you feel/touch? What can you hear? And what can you taste? Focusing on each of your five main senses will often help you feel more grounded, more alive, and more present in the moment.

Quotes – A very simple yet effective instant help tip is to read a quote. It can put things in perspective, give you inspiration, take your mind off the problems, and provide a comfort to you when anxious. You may have some favourite quotes you know and can recall or carry a notebook of quotes or have some listed on your phone, for example, so they are on hand if needed.

Think of other techniques that might work for you and try them out. The more options you have, the better, and why not ask friends for suggestions and what they might do?

'You can't stop the waves but you can learn to surf.'

CHAPTER 5 SUMMARY

As you can see there are many more areas to consider, to understand and to see how they affect you and how you can make changes to help yourself overcome the anxiety.

There are also a few instant help tips that are worth trying out and you may be able to think of your own or get some suggestions from friends that haven't been mentioned here. The more knowledge, understanding, tools, techniques and tips you have then you will feel more in control and thus less anxious – so keep building upon this.

You should be finding that many of the positive and productive actions you are taking are having additional knock on benefits so the more you keep doing this, the more benefits will keep on coming.

Chapter 6
Anxiety, Stress & Control

Objectives:
This chapter will look at stress in relation to anxiety, the need for control and perspective, plus fears and phobias. You will get more understanding and knowledge and there is a technique to apply so you can regain control and become calm when anxious thoughts start up.

Anxiety, stress, and phobias

Anxiety can cause stress, and stress can cause anxiety. There are many similarities with the two conditions and also some major differences. So let's take a closer look at stress first:

Stress

The official dictionary definition of stress is:
'A state of mental or emotional strain or tension resulting from adverse or demanding circumstances'
Another definition which I often use is as follows:
'A stressful circumstance is one with which you cannot cope successfully (or believe you cannot cope) and which results in unwanted physical, mental, or emotional reactions'
It is important to recognise and remember that sometimes stress can be a good thing. Often small amounts of stress in the right circumstances can be very beneficial as it can make us more focused and more disciplined, and our adrenaline levels may increase, helping us concentrate and perform to a high level. However, unless controlled and managed properly, stress will

usually cause unwanted characteristics and symptoms which will continue to get worse if nothing is done.

There are many characteristics and symptoms of stress, and although you would expect many of these to occur as a reaction to a particular event, there is a big difference between stress and a normal reaction to one-off situations. Stress will usually build up, often quite slowly, and the gap between your symptoms at the outset and where they are now is significantly wider, although you may not be aware of how wide that gap has become. Here are some responses by individuals when asked the question, **'What symptoms, behaviours, and characteristics do you associate with stress?'**

- Loss of confidence and low self-esteem. Feeling numb and not valued. Inability to sleep and tiredness despite a full night's sleep. Loss of appetite or cravings for sugar, caffeine, or alcohol. Irritable and negative thought patterns. Withdrawal from friends generally, even though you've previously enjoyed social occasions.
- Anxiety, overwhelming feeling of being out of control, panic, irrational behaviour – not having a clear head to deal with the challenges you are facing. Disjointed sleep patterns, loss of concentration and focus.
- Stress can cause many negative and destructive emotions and behaviours. Often a feeling of anxiety which leads to irrational and runaway thoughts. Tension throughout the body, shallow breathing, excess perspiration, inability to relax, constant worrying and agitation. Being unable to focus on anything other than the tormenting, catastrophic thoughts, and leading to an ever-expanding circle of negativity.
- Anxiety, being short-tempered, irritable and impatient. Not listening to reason, withdrawal, and having negative emotions.
- Symptoms of stress include poor concentration, anxiety, and lacking motivation to be able to tackle the tasks you face. Behaviours and

characteristics associated with stress could be a loss of appetite, having mood swings and snapping at people, lack of sleep, being unable to sort/prioritise workloads/tasks.

- Feeling overwhelmed and unable to cope with increasing pressures. Getting frustrated, irritable, impatient, upset and angry. Feeling tired and tense so unable to relax and switch off.

A useful way of looking at stress and the effect it has is by breaking it down into stages. Stress will usually build up over quite a period of time and the person directly affected may not recognise the real damage and risks unless they step back and look at the different stages. Here is a familiar pattern and breakdown of stress:

Stage 1 – In the first stage you may find yourself feeling overworked, uncertain of your own abilities, but reluctant to take days off.

Stage 2 – In the second stage you may find yourself tired, irritated and frustrated, working long hours but seeming to achieve less. You may be skipping meals, or 'comfort eating'.

Stage 3 – In the third stage you may feel resentful or guilty, you will probably be neglecting your family and friends, and will no longer be enjoying work or life.

Stage 4 – Finally you may withdraw completely, succumb to illness, or drug or alcohol abuse, feel like a failure or completely break down emotionally and mentally.

Even in the earliest stages it is important to recognise stress and seek to manage it and control it as much as possible. It is far too easy, once on the path towards stress, to stay on it and for matters to build up and get worse, and the further down the path the harder it is to change course. So take time to reflect and think about your own personal situation, your stress levels and what you can do to manage those effectively.

What causes stress?

Everyone has a different set of circumstances in their life, with different factors that affect them and different ways of dealing with and managing those factors. A factor that affects one person will not affect another, at least not in the same way, so it is important to understand the differences and apply them to yourself. Think about all the factors and areas of your life that you feel create and build stress for you. Write down a list and then as far as you can try to put them in order of those that affect you the most and cause the most stress.

Here are some responses from people when asked the question, **'What main things and factors cause stress in your life?'**

- People – partners, family members, work colleagues. Situations – money, health, work or parenting issues.
- External factors beyond your control like health issues.
- Work – when people let you down and don't deliver what they say they will, creating more pressure for you. Friends who don't support you as you would hope when you are experiencing a difficult time in your life.
- Money causes stress. Work – too much of it and not enough people to cope with it. Moving home or buying a house. Loss of control in

personal and work life.

- Financial worries, relationship problems, pressure at work, not having time to exercise or do the things I want to do. People who are rude or inconsiderate and letting me down.

There are a wide range of factors that can cause stress in people's lives and have a negative effect on them. However, many of these factors are very difficult to prevent. So many issues are caused by other people or events where the individual affected has no control and cannot change the situation. There is so much dependence on another person doing something the way you would like, and when they don't you become more stressed. So much of your stress and how it causes problems for you is not within your control. Therefore if you can't change what happens you must try to focus on how it affects you and how you deal with those factors. Remember stress is your reaction to something, so no matter what the 'something' is, you can be in control of how much it affects you and how much damage it causes. You have to learn to manage your reaction to those factors that cause stress.

Stress-related depression

Generally speaking, if you asked any group of people, whether that was in a work environment or the general public, if they had ever been stressed or were stressed, or even do they suffer from stress, many people would say yes. Often they would laugh about it and say, "Yes, I'm always stressed and life is stressful, who isn't stressed?" The reaction tends to be one of not taking stress too seriously and people feel relatively comfortable admitting to feelings of stress. It doesn't seem to be something people are ashamed of or embarrassed about, and they will admit to stress.

However, if you asked the same groups if they had ever had depression, were depressed or were suffering from depression, then very often the answers and reactions would be very different. Significantly fewer people would admit to having depression and there would be no laughter or amusing reactions. The general response would be more muted, less admission and a little bit of unease. People tend not to recognise or admit to depression, often feeling ashamed or embarrassed by the word.

Yet stress and depression are so often linked. Stress can be a major factor in depression and the characteristics and symptoms go hand in hand. A very common form of depression is the stress-related or stress-induced type, and it is vital that people recognise this and understand the link. Once understood, it is very possible to manage stress, which in turn will prevent depression.

I have learned over the last few years how to manage stress effectively and prevent any depression occurring. I have also learned and understood how the build-up of stress and the way I used to deal with stress-causing factors caused my own personal stress-related depression. I suffered from many of the symptoms of depression without really understanding or knowing what was happening to me or why I felt the way I did. Through extensive research, reading, and thinking, I understood that I had been exposed to huge amounts of stress and combined with my type of personality it was almost inevitable that depression would result.

However, once the strong link between stress and depression is understood, then you can begin to work out the best and most effective ways of reducing stress and managing situations so that you can deal with anything, and depression in this respect is always preventable. The underlying causes may always be there but you can manage the effect and put in place the techniques and use the tools so that you can be 100% confident that depression will never result as a consequence of not managing your stress.

Curse of the strong

A book I read a few years ago, and one I would strongly recommend to anyone who feels they may be suffering from stress-related depression, is called *Depressive Illness: The Curse of the Strong* by Dr Tim Cantopher. Essentially the book explains how a certain type of person can become ill from depression caused by stress. That person would usually be viewed by themselves and others as 'strong', the type of person who has great qualities, achieves a lot, whom people look up to and admire, is determined and successful. In fact they have many very favourable and welcome characteristics, although in addition they have others that are also mentioned below in this list:

Personality characteristics:

- (Moral) strength
- Reliability
- Diligence
- Strong conscience
- Strong sense of responsibility
- A tendency to focus on the needs of others before one's own
- Sensitivity
- Vulnerability to criticism
- Self-esteem dependent on the evaluation of others

So basically if you are this type of person then you are actually quite vulnerable to getting depressed as a result of stress build-up, and a large percentage of people who suffer from depression fall into this category. A very good way of summing this up is as follows:

Give a set of stresses to someone who is weak, cynical or lazy and he will quickly give up, so he will never get stressed enough to become ill. A strong person, on the other hand, will react to these pressures by trying to overcome them. After all, he has overcome every challenge he has faced in the past through diligence and effort.

Fill in the table below with, on the left-hand side, examples of things that increase your stress levels, and on the right examples of things you can do that would lower your stress levels.

Examples of what causes you stress	Examples of what can reduce your stress
e.g. Getting PPI-related phone calls and texts	e.g. Go for a walk at lunchtime
Driving – traffic, middle-lane motorway drivers, people who don't signal, too slow drivers, tail-gaters, etc.	Have a long, hot shower

Stress and Anxiety

Clearly stress in itself can be unpleasant, debilitating and unhealthy. It can also lead to depression, as discussed above. And it can also cause anxiety problems both in terms of initiating them and increasing them.

If you become stressed about something then it is likely to lead to an emotional arousal and various stress hormones are released into the body. It is your body's natural way to try and help deal with a perceived threat. For example, your heart rate will increase and your breathing may become quicker and you will feel on edge, with a heightened sense of awareness. These kinds of changes are generally going to aid you in any kind of physical threat or where you need to physically respond because that was the main kind of threat that humans faced over hundreds of thousands of years.

However, in modern times, most of the stress we have is not related to physical threats and our natural response with the release of stress hormones is usually not helpful to us. A faster heartbeat, quick breathing, and release of adrenaline may have helped us fight off a wild animal many thousands of years ago but it doesn't help much when the stress is about delivering a presentation at work on Tuesday morning. In fact, it will typically make things much worse and will create additional anxiety.

Stress can affect us in many ways including with our thinking, emotions, behaviours, and our physical health and wellbeing. Anxiety can cause the same issues, and combined they make things even worse.

Anxiety, Control & Perspective

The key to reducing your anxiety is to feel you have control over any threats, challenges, or situations. The more you don't have control or feel you don't have the control, the more your anxiety is likely to increase. If you believe you can control a 'threat' then you will certainly be less anxious.

Control can be achieved in two fundamental ways. Firstly, if you can have a real and direct influence yourself over the situation so that you can prevent the threat occurring; and secondly, that you can cope and deal with any threat if it was to happen.

Real and direct influence over potential threat

If you are confident in yourself, your abilities, and your skills, then you are likely to believe that you can influence situations that could be threats to you and then stop those threats from happening. If you go through your life believing that you can prevent threats occurring, then you are less likely to feel anxious about what could happen. Your confidence in yourself means you feel in control and can influence your life and events so you have no need to worry and be anxious.

Therefore, working on building your confidence is really important, and there is a lot you can do to increase this, and therefore not only will you feel better through improved confidence, you will also feel better due to less anxiety.

Cope and deal with any threat

If you believe that you will be able to cope and deal with any threats that do occur, then you will worry much less about them and therefore your anxiety in relation to these will decrease significantly. Nearly all people who have anxiety issues do not believe they will be able to cope well with the situations and threats and instead focus on all the negatives around the dangers, what will happen and what will go wrong.

If you believe that you have the abilities, skills, and resources to cope with the events and respond positively, then there is no need to be anxious. Again this comes down to confidence in yourself and also knowing that you have coped well with past experiences.

However, the more you worry about not being able to cope, the more anxious you will become and the more likely you won't cope well with any real threat. The anxiety then magnifies the issue and it becomes a vicious circle as you then don't cope well and your fears are confirmed.

Identify past experiences you have had that have caused anxiety or stress	How did you deal with these situations and what could you have done differently to help?

It is very likely that with any examples you have given in the above table you managed to survive and get through them. They were most likely not as bad as you feared and you dealt with them and coped with anything negative that occurred. So it was actually ok. In the future not only do you have the knowledge that you have coped and dealt with many situations in the past, but now you have more tools and techniques to use in order to cope even better! You can deal with anything and cope effectively, so you must remember this and remind yourself whenever you get any anxious thoughts. You can deal with any threat and you will be ok. In fact you will be more than ok!

Rational thinking and perspective

Generally the more anxious anyone gets, the less rational, logical and clear is their thinking. They lose focus and perspective, and whatever the thing is they are getting anxious about is magnified and they become fixated on that thing with tunnel-like vision. Their expectation is one of a negative outcome and they are anticipating that a scary, horrible, dangerous and difficult situation will occur. This negative focus and build-up cause greater anxiety and the lack of rational and clear thinking also creates more anxiety.

Think about a horror film and how a good director will look to build up the anticipation with the use of music, scenery, skilled actors and that all-important suspense. The viewer is focused more and more on what may happen, building up the anticipation with tunnel-like vision and waiting for the scary thing to happen. The combination of different anticipatory factors makes it scary. If you were to watch the same film without sound and you knew what was going to happen it wouldn't be scary at all.

What you must try to do is regain perspective and think rationally and clearly and believe the outcome will be ok. Of course, for someone who has anxiety and has consistently thought this way for a long time, it will be hard to do, but it is very achievable. When you sense that anxiety building, you have to step back and gain perspective on the situation and pause and take a deep breath so you can think more clearly and rationally.

As an example, take a famous painting like *Sunflowers* by Vincent van Gogh, and imagine it framed on a wall in a gallery. If you were to go right up close to within a few centimetres and focus on the middle of the painting you would just see an unattractive, blurred, coloured mess. Yet, if you step back a few paces the painting would reveal itself and it would become clear what it was and how beautiful it is. If you can do the same in an anxiety-related moment then things will look very different and much clearer. You can then think more rationally and things will make more sense and you can regain the all-important perspective.

Fears and phobias

Many people have phobias which are essentially the same as fears but they have a more severe impact on someone's life. We only have two natural fears which are the fear of loud noise and the fear of falling, and all our other fears are somehow learned or picked up in some way, unnaturally, during our lives. Nearly all fears and phobias are from poor thinking or rather a belief we have which is wrong.

Many people will say their fears come from real traumas and experiences they have had and in some cases this will be true. However, probably the most common fear is that of flying and yet hardly anyone has had a real-life flying trauma. So where does this fear or phobia come from?

In nearly all cases it is due to the person having a lack of control combined with not believing they can influence the situation or cope with any issue. So they feel vulnerable and have a very negative thinking style in relation to this lack of control. Their answer is to avoid the situation at all costs as that way nothing bad can happen. They build up in their head all the possible disasters and terrible things that could happen with no sense of rational thinking or perspective.

The way to overcome these fears and phobias is to gain perspective, think rationally and get an internal sense of thinking whereby they believe they can either influence the situation or cope if needed to, and therefore they have control. The best way to do this is to do whatever it is they are fearful of and have it proven that it is ok and keep doing it so that the fear and anxiety continue to decrease.

The DREAM technique

This comes from a book I would recommend called *Thrive* by Rob Kelly and it is a practical technique to help try to eliminate those unwanted thoughts and actions that build up, causing anxiety and associated issues. Like with any technique it is important to understand what it is trying to do and then you must apply it fully and keep practising. If you do then it will become easier to do and it will work!

This technique is particularly useful as it is not only straightforward but you can perform it at any time and in any situation when needed.
The actions that make up **DREAM** are as follows:
Detect: Detect that you are having an anxious thought or build-up.
Reward: Reward yourself for detecting the unhelpful thoughts.
Escape: Escape from the situation that brought on the anxiety. **Amend**: Amend the thoughts to create a new positive one. **Magnify**: Magnify this positive thought as much as possible.

In more detail let's go through each stage of the process:

Detect – You need to be as self-aware as possible, and recognise when you start to have an unhelpful and anxious thought. Detect it as early as possible so that it doesn't build up too much. It will become easier to detect earlier the more you practise. Basically you are detecting any negative, unhelpful, worrying, anxious-type thought and when you do make sure you stop. Stop right there and say no to that thought.

Reward – So once you have detected the negative thought and stopped what you were doing, you should now congratulate yourself. Praise and reward yourself for both detecting the problem and then stopping it. Pat yourself on the back and thank yourself because you have done something that is really important and is going to really help you.

Escape – You now need to remove yourself from the situation as much as you can, especially if the situation was a factor in the start of the negative thoughts and anxiety. If you can, go and do something different and something that will make you feel in control and positive. Make the choice to remove yourself from a potentially bad place to a good one, and recognise that you have that choice and the power to do so.

Amend – This is where you go back to the unhelpful and negative thought and look to rationalise it and amend it to a more helpful and positive thought. Because you have stepped back and can view it clearer and in a more rational way you can now consider it in a different light. Take control of the thought and focus on the positives and how the situation can be much better.

Magnify – Now that you have revisited the original thought and anxiety in a different and more rational and positive way, you should look to magnify this further and make it even better. Really focus on creating a very positive image and exaggerate this to make it incredibly strong, powerful, and bright. The bigger and more positive this new image is, the better.

Try this technique out and really focus on each element and keep practising so it becomes easier and more likely to work effectively in any situation for any reason so you can get back to a calm and more relaxed state.

CHAPTER 6 SUMMARY

Often anxiety is linked to stress and depression, and although all three conditions are separate and are issues in their own right, it is very common to have strong links with both causes and effects associated with all three. so being aware of this and how each relate is important and can help you to understand better, and then overcome, your anxiety. we have also looked at the importance of gaining control and having influence over your everyday life, which is improved by rational thinking, a sense of perspective and techniques to ensure this happens.

Each day you are gaining more control and influence over your situation, and the more you continue to practise, the better it will be.

Chapter 7
Building Your Defences

Objectives:

This chapter is all about your defences, your resilience, and your ability to deal with and manage any problems. It is often said that it is less important what happens to you and much more important how you handle it and react to it. So let's build up those defences, become more resilient, and feel confident in our ability to deal with anything that life has to throw at us going forward.

Your defences and dealing with the bad days

Building upon everything you have already learned, read through the following sections that will help you to further grow your defences and help you deal much better with any setbacks and bad days you experience. Do not let the occasional negative piece of news, or annoying person, or unfair event cause you to dip on your journey to overcoming anxiety.

Bad days are inevitable and normal

Everyone, no matter who they are, will experience bad days in their life, and sometimes for no obvious reason. Often the bad days are a direct result of certain events, circumstances, experiences, or people doing or saying something you don't like. There is also the possibility of misunderstandings, an overreaction or even the expectation that you will have a bad day actually creating a bad day due to the negative thinking.

Some bad days are inevitable and normal, and you cannot go through life without some bad days. However, firstly you need to ensure that you minimise these bad days as much as you can and then when they do happen you deal with them effectively. So, in addition to all the previous chapters, here are some key areas to ensure you do have strong defences and can deal with those bad days.

Get the facts

It is so important, wherever possible, to get the facts with regard to anything that affects you and may cause a bad day and increase your anxiety. You hear some bad news, someone says something you don't like, that letter or email doesn't arrive, you don't get a reply to a text you sent or you start to feel unwell. So many examples of things that can happen to you where you jump to conclusions and make assumptions in a negative way which has an effect on your mood and how you are dealing with your anxiety.

In many of these cases you will not have all the facts and the reality is different from what you presume. Your presumptions can set you back and cause additional issues. However, if you make sure as much as you can that you have all the facts first, then you will be in a much stronger position because you will wait for the facts and the reality. And the reality is likely, quite often, to not be as bad.

So as a way of dealing with bad days and building your defences, make sure you always wait or look to get all the facts before you react or think the worse. Get into that habit and you will be much stronger and more resilient.

Mistakes and misunderstandings happen

There will be times when you will make a mistake or misunderstand something and so will everybody else. Nobody is perfect and for many reasons these mistakes and misunderstandings can happen that may cause some issues to you. It could be that you get angry, annoyed and upset with yourself as a result or you may have those feelings related to someone else.

If you allow it, then these inevitable but unintentional mistakes and misunderstandings could cause you further problems. Your anger could build, your mood dip lower, you may do or say something you regret and your defences could be weakened because of the way you handle the situation. So instead remember that mistakes and misunderstandings happen all the time and are usually unintentional. Don't be so hard on yourself or other people who are responsible and recognise that these things will always happen, and if you can react in a pragmatic, rational, and empathetic way then it will be much better for you and you can remain strong with your defences intact.

Negative expectations

For many people, when suffering from anxiety, they will often have negative thoughts that relate to the past, the present, and the future. Their expectations will be more negative and therefore they will live their life anticipating negative things happening to them which heightens the anxiety. Unfortunately this is common and can have a big impact on how quickly someone overcomes their anxiety and how strong their defences are in preventing it going forward.

If you expect a negative life, then you are more likely to obtain that. You will be more susceptible to negative experiences and thoughts and you will be weaker as a result. So the less negative your expectations, the better, and indeed the more positive your expectations, then that will be better still.

Your defences will be stronger and you will deal better with future events and situations if your expectations are more positive. That is a mindset and something you can control. It may not be easy and will require effort and practice, but you will be in a much better position if you focus on positive thinking and expectations rather than having the unhelpful and damaging negative expectations.

Everything is temporary

It is worth knowing that pretty much everything in life is temporary – and that includes both the good things and the bad things. Having that knowledge can be very beneficial. With regard to the good stuff, you are more likely to embrace it, to enjoy it more, to value it and to not take it for granted. And when it comes to the bad stuff, you know that it won't last.

When you are going through difficult periods, having bad days, when things are going against you, when life isn't fair and you are in despair, remember it is only temporary. Things will change, good stuff will happen, you will receive some good news and get that break you want – it is inevitable. You don't know what the future holds or what is round the corner, so just because you are having a bad day, bad week, or bad month it doesn't mean that good stuff won't happen soon.

There are so many people I know and whom I have talked to when they have been in despair, feeling like there is no hope and can't see how anything good will happen to them. Yet, in all cases, down the line things have changed and good things have happened. Perhaps that has been several months later but it has happened and they always say that for anyone going through similar to what they were, then they have to remember that the pain, anguish and despair are only temporary.

Use that knowledge to be patient, have belief, and to be more resilient to the challenges life throws at you.

'Everything in life is temporary. So if things are going good, enjoy it, and if things are going bad, don't worry, it can't last forever.'

Rocky quote and boxing analogy

Many of you would have heard of the actor Sylvester Stallone and the *Rocky* films he wrote, directed, and starred in about a boxer who triumphed over adversity. In the sixth and final film of the series, called *Rocky Balboa*, there is a scene where the boxer is talking to his grown-up son during an argument and I believe there are several very poignant and important messages he gets across. This has become one of my favourite quotes, or rather, series of quotes. Here it is:

"Then the time came for you to be your own man and take on the world, and you did. But somewhere along the line, you changed. You stopped being you. You let people stick a finger in your face and tell you you're no good. And when things got hard, you started looking for something to blame, like a big shadow. Let me tell you something you already know. The world ain't all sunshine and rainbows. It's a very mean and nasty place and I don't care how tough you are, it will beat you to your knees and keep you there permanently if you let it. You, me, or nobody is going to hit as hard as life. But it ain't about how hard you hit. It's about how hard you can get hit and keep moving forward. How much you can take and keep moving forward. That's how winning is done! Now if you know what you're worth then go out and get what you're worth. But you've got to be willing to take the hits, and not pointing fingers saying you ain't where you want to be because of him, or her, or anybody! Cowards do that and that ain't you! You're better than that! I'm always going to love you no matter what. No matter what happens. You're my son and you're my blood. You're the best thing in my life. But until you start believing in yourself, you ain't going to have a life."

There are several good points and things to consider above, but one of the key ones is about the fact that it's not about how hard you hit but how you deal with getting hit. You need good defences, and all the best boxers will focus more on their defence than their attacks. Being able to avoid the hits, block the hits and if necessary absorb the hits is key to victory. And in life you will succeed if you have strong defences.

If you can develop your defences it will give you great strength, courage, and confidence because you will start to realise that no matter what life throws at you and no matter how hard it hits, you can take it. You can avoid, block or absorb those hits. You can take whatever comes your way. You will realise that although at times it's uncomfortable and you would rather not be receiving those hits, they do not hurt you or weaken you, and they actually make you stronger.

Visualise being in a boxing ring and life is throwing all these punches at you, yet you can take it and you know that your defences are stronger than anything that life can hit you with. What a great feeling knowing you can deal with it and you won't lose, and also the fact your time will come when you can start throwing some hits back, and ultimately you are going to succeed and come out victorious.

Sense of humour

It is very easy while suffering from anxiety to lose our sense of humour, and understandably so. When you feel anxious and are often thinking negatively it is hard to laugh and joke and see the funny side of things. However, it is really important to laugh, joke, have some fun, watch comedy, have some banter, and smile! We want to enjoy our lives more and be happier, and we are all capable of laughter and we can enjoy laughing even if we may not feel in a particularly jolly, laughter-inducing mood. It is often in those times when we need to make the effort to find our sense of humour.

There are so many things that can and do make us laugh, so seek those out. It could be a comedy programme, a funny film, some jokes you find on the Internet, watching funny clips on YouTube, meeting up with friends for some banter and telling stories, doing some silly dancing or pulling funny faces in front of the mirror. There are so many things that you can do to bring some laughter to your life, and the benefits from improving

your mood are worth that effort, and a sense of humour is a great way to build up your defences and to relax more and worry less.

Plus it is vital that you can still laugh at yourself, too. Allow yourself to laugh. Don't feel guilty about having some fun, smiling, and laughing, and if you find yourself in a situation where you are stressing yourself out and worrying out of control, then to step back and laugh at yourself can be hugely beneficial.

Learn to dance in the rain

There are many uncertainties in life but there are also many certainties, like the fact that life will always throw up challenges for us to deal with. Also, everyone is different, with different circumstances, abilities, skills, and opportunities, but again that is life. You may be disadvantaged in some way, you may have some bad luck, things may go against you and life may seem unfair. But a great quote that recognises this and also recognises that it is your life and you only get one shot at it is "you don't have to wait for the storm to pass if you learn to dance in the rain".

Try to make the most of your circumstances, your skills, your situation, and your abilities. Nothing is perfect and the rain will fall at times, so get out there and dance in that rain. If every day was warm and sunny with blue skies, then you would soon stop appreciating it and life would become quite boring. Embrace and appreciate those sunny days and make the most of them, but don't let the dark days stop you living your life. Learn to deal with the challenges and the inevitable difficulties that arise in life and that way your life will be a whole lot better and more rewarding for you and others.

You will be so much stronger from this experience

In some ways having anxiety is a blessing – because once you overcome it you have so much more strength and power knowing that nothing ever again can be so bad – and if you can overcome the anxiety issues, then you can succeed at anything.

You might not recognise this now, but in the future it is likely that you will reflect on your issues and come to the conclusion that you are a stronger and better person as a result of your experiences. You no longer have to fear anything as you know you can deal with whatever comes your way. You will have so much less stress and worry in your life and much more time and energy to spend on positive and productive things that will enhance your life. You will also be better placed to help others and make a real difference to other people's lives.

The actor Michael J. Fox (the *Back to the Future* guy!) was diagnosed with Parkinson's disease in his early thirties at the height of his success in the film and TV industry yet he called his autobiography *Lucky Man*. This was because on reflection he believed that getting the disease when he did was a huge blessing and made his life so much better. Now that sounds crazy on the face of it, yet his explanation was that for many years prior to his illness he was an arrogant, rude, selfish alcoholic who treated people really badly and was basically not a nice person. The diagnosis was a massive wake-up call and changed his life completely to one where he stopped drinking, treated people with respect, gained humility, focused on helping others, and became a much better person. He saw himself as being lucky to have been able to change his life around as a result of Parkinson's disease.

In a similar way it is possible that in the future you will consider yourself lucky to have had the experience of anxiety and come through it. Remember that!

Now complete the below table using some of your own examples:

Examples of situations in the past where you have experienced anxiety and what happened to you.	In the same situation write down what you would now do and how you would deal with the situation from what you have learned.
e.g. you get caught in a long traffic delay on the way to work and you have a busy day ahead including some important meetings – you panic, worry, get upset and angry, and your heart races and your breathing is hard to control. You get so worked up and start thinking of all the consequences and worst-case scenarios.	e.g. you would realise that it is not your fault and you cannot do anything about it. You don't panic as you recognise that won't be helpful. You think rationally and methodically about how you can manage the rest of the working day and you even put on some music and have a singalong in the car!

Treatments

I have focused very much on understanding yourself and how you can help yourself to reduce, manage, and prevent anxiety and related issues, and I strongly believe this is the best way to be successful in the short, medium, and long term with such conditions. There is so much you can do to help the situation, starting with understanding what it is, who you are, and how the two relate.

There are also other things that you can do or try in the way of treatments, and this section looks at some of these options. Some may work and some may not, so be aware that there is never one solution for everyone, and what may be really beneficial for one person may not help someone else. Try to understand as much as possible about each option and why it may be helpful and how it might work. Seek information, ask questions, try to understand, get advice and explore the different options. And wherever possible ensure that any treatment is regulated, approved, recommended, and delivered by professionals and that you are not being exploited.

Medication

It is always advisable to speak with your doctor if you feel the need and would like advice on options available, including medication. I would always encourage people to try and understand as much as possible about their issues and factors, and what can work best, and explore all potential options. This could include medication which your doctor might prescribe you. There are four types of medication which are commonly used and might be beneficial in managing anxiety:

- Antidepressants
- Beta blockers
- Tranquillisers (benzodiazepines)
- Pregabalin (an anticonvulsant drug)

According to the National Institute for Health and Care Excellence (NICE) – the organisation that produces health care guidelines – ideally your doctor should offer you other kinds of treatment for anxiety first, before prescribing these drugs.

Antidepressants

Antidepressants might help you feel calmer and more able to benefit from a more long-term treatment such as a talking treatment.

However, they can sometimes cause unwanted side effects, such as increasing your anxiety, increasing feelings of depression, or causing problems with sleeping.

Beta blockers

Beta blockers, such as propranolol, can treat some of the physical symptoms of anxiety, including a rapid heartbeat, palpitations and tremors (shaking).

They can be helpful when you have to face a particular phobia, such as going on an aeroplane.

However, they are not psychiatric medication, so they won't reduce any of your psychological symptoms.

Tranquillisers

Your doctor might prescribe you tranquillisers (benzodiazepines) if your anxiety is very severe or disabling.

Tranquillisers can't tackle the cause of your problems, but they can bring some relief until you have another form of treatment in place.

Tranquillisers should only be a temporary measure, because it's possible that you could become addicted to these drugs and have difficulty coming off them.

Pregabalin (an anticonvulsant drug)

In some cases, such as if you have a diagnosis of generalised anxiety disorder (GAD), your doctor may decide to prescribe you a drug called pregabalin (Lyrica).

This drug is an anticonvulsant medication which is normally used to treat epilepsy, but is also licensed to treat anxiety.

Cognitive Behavioural Therapy (CBT)

Cognitive behavioural therapy (CBT) is one of the most effective treatments for General Anxiety Disorder (GAD). Studies of different treatments for GAD have found that the benefits of CBT may last longer than those of medication, although no single treatment is best for everyone so it is important to look at different treatments to find out what works best for you.

CBT aims to help you to understand how your problems, thoughts, feelings and behaviour affect each other. It can also help you to question your negative and anxious thoughts, and do things you would usually avoid because they make you anxious.

CBT will usually involve meeting with a specially trained and accredited therapist for a one-hour session every week for three to four months. Any therapist who delivers CBT should be qualified and registered, and use a standardised treatment so make sure any courses you attend or therapists you use are official, and a first step is probably to ask your doctor for recommendations.

Mindfulness

Mindfulness is an integrative, mind-body-based approach that can help you manage your thoughts and feelings, and change the way you relate to experiences. It is becoming more common as a preventative method for people who experience issues of depression and anxiety, and even though it is understood to have Buddhist origins, you don't need to be religious or spiritual to practise mindfulness.

The primary aim is to help us to pay attention specifically to the present moment using techniques like meditation, breathing and yoga. Through practice it can help us become more aware of our thoughts, feelings, and body sensations so that instead of being overwhelmed by them, we're better able to manage them. It can give us more insight into our emotions, boost attention and concentration, and improve relationships.

Anyone can potentially benefit from mindfulness and it can be practised in person, either through a group course or one-to-one with a trained mindfulness coach. There are also online courses, books and audio, too, where you can learn through self-directed practice at home.

Support groups

Anxiety issues can often make people feel isolated and reclusive, plus many feel that other people do not understand, or cannot relate to, their issues. So being able to attend a support group where they are other people with potentially similar issues to meet and talk with may be very helpful.

An increased level of empathy in a safe environment should help people feel more relaxed, and being able to talk about issues in this way could be effective and there may be good advice on offer from other members of the group or from the facilitator.

Such support groups will normally be organised by charities or local health organisations. So ask your doctor if they have any contacts or research yourself to see if any exist in your area. Charities like MIND, Anxiety UK, Rethink, and Depression Alliance may help.

Applied relaxation

Applied relaxation is an alternative type of psychological treatment that can be as effective as CBT in treating General Anxiety Disorder (GAD). Applied relaxation focuses on relaxing your muscles in a particular way during situations that usually cause anxiety. The technique needs to be taught by a trained therapist, but generally involves:

- Learning how to relax your muscles
- Learning how to relax your muscles quickly and in response to a trigger, such as the word 'relax'
- Practising relaxing your muscles in situations that make you anxious

As with CBT, applied relaxation therapy will usually mean meeting with a therapist for a one-hour session every week for three to four months.

Hypnotherapy

Hypnotherapy is the use of hypnosis for the treatment and alleviation of a variety of physical and psychological symptoms. Hypnosis aims to allow the patient to experience often quite deep levels of relaxation and so helps to reduce levels of stress and anxiety in this respect.

Additionally, it is often used alongside classical behavioural therapies such as 'systematic desensitisation' which focuses on specific worries to an individual. Two important elements of this therapy are the ability to clearly imagine something that makes you feel anxious, and then to attain a deeply relaxed state. Hypnosis helps to achieve both of these more easily and quickly than many other forms of treatment and may be a series of sessions or potentially just a one-off session.

Acupuncture

Acupuncture originated in China and has been in use for more than 2,000 years, with practitioners claiming that by inserting tiny needles into specific areas of the skin, they can affect the meridians, or channels of pain, that run up and down the body, blocking pain.

Research has shown that acupuncture may also help ease anxiety by acting on areas of the brain known to reduce sensitivity to pain and stress, as well as promoting relaxation and deactivating the areas of the brain which are responsible for feelings of anxiety and worry.

The fact that you generally lie still and quietly in a relaxed environment, usually for 30–40 minutes, is on its own likely to help relax you and reduce anxiety, plus there is the potential for a placebo effect. Generally people will use acupuncture over a series of sessions.

CHAPTER 7 SUMMARY

This penultimate chapter has focused on your defences and resilience, plus a range of potential treatments that are available to help overcome anxiety. You need to have a strong defence because life can be tough and can throw all sorts of issues at you. However, with a strong defence built on your improved knowledge, understanding, tools and techniques you can feel confident in being able to deal with anything, and your anxiety can become a thing of the past. I believe that you are the best person to deal with and overcome anxiety; however, it is definitely worth looking at other treatments as well and some may be very beneficial for you.

Well done on how far you have come so far and the effort you have put in – now keep going into the final chapter.

Chapter 8
Keep Learning & Doing the Right Things

Objectives:
Your final chapter of the book is all about recapping on what you have learned and understood, using the tools and techniques you have acquired, utilising your toolbox, keep practising and using the knowledge you now have and realising you are now in control of your ship!

Words and language used

The words and language that you use can have a big effect on your thoughts and actions even if you don't consciously realise it. If you speak and think negative words you will undoubtedly lower your mood, anticipate negative outcomes, increase your anxiety, make yourself stressed, and feel powerless to control and influence a situation. If you use positive words you will feel more powerful, anticipate positive outcomes, reduce anxiety, create less stress, and feel more confident in what you are doing. As well as using positive words it is important to use active language, as it empowers you and suggests you are able to take control and influence your situation. Our language can impact upon our beliefs so using positive and active words will help you to believe you can deal with everything. In contrast, if you use negative, dramatic, or sensationalist language you are likely to increase your anxiety and feel out of control. So think carefully about your language and words you use and endeavour to use more positive and active ones – it will make a difference!

Keep learning and doing the right things

The main thing I have learned about issues such as anxiety and depression from lots of research and speaking to many others is that although it is very beatable, you have to keep learning and doing the right things in order to prevent it returning. Far too many people who manage to overcome their issues then fail to manage themselves going forward, and similar issues return. It is unfortunate but it is also a reality that people stop doing the things that work and default back to old habits and become complacent, and the anxiety and/or depression returns. Make sure that does not happen to you.

It is likely that you are more susceptible or predisposed to these conditions than many other people, and so it is essential that you recognise any signals, triggers, or circumstances that may affect you and ensure you do all those things that you know will work. Use those tools and techniques. If you keep practising, seek to understand yourself even more and do the right things, then you will always be able to prevent issues coming back. For example, although I have never really suffered directly from anxiety, I have had depression, yet I am now 100% confident that I will never suffer from depression again due to my improved knowledge and understanding, combined with being skilled in the use of those tools and techniques that work for me. You can be the same.

Keep using your toolbox

I hope you have been using your toolbox! It really is a very powerful thing if used well. You should never be in a position where you cannot do something to improve the situation. Whenever you need to you can go to your toolbox and take something out to use there and then to help.

The spiral of decline should become a thing of the past because now, and going forward, as soon as you recognise a downward shift in your mood, thoughts, feelings and behaviour you can push it back up again by using your toolbox. What a powerful thing it is to have that control where you can use your tools in any situation to improve things, and the more you practise and the wider range of tools you have, the better and easier it will be. Keep adding new things to your toolbox, trying new possible tools out, replacing things if they need replacing, or upgrading to better tools!

What works for some people won't work for others, and on some days there will be tools that aren't that effective, for whatever reason, but on other days they are ideal. It is also helpful to keep your toolbox organised so you know what you have and where they are so you can easily find them whenever you need to.

Write down here all the tools in your toolbox – including the ones you use regularly and also ones that perhaps you don't use often and even those you have yet to use:

Internal vs. external

Remember how important it is to be more internal in your thinking and behaviour so that you have a greater sense of power, control, and influence over your life. This will increase your confidence, provide more certainty, and empower you. It is your life where you are the one most responsible for what you do and how you do it.

The more external you think, then the more disempowering this is and the greater uncertainty there will be for you. Your life shouldn't be controlled by luck, fate, other people, superstition, horoscopes, Tarot cards, or wishful thinking. You should control your life as much as possible and you can be in control. Believe in yourself, take responsibility, be who you are and be the captain of your own ship.

Understand who you are

We are all different, with varying genetics, upbringings, environments, and experiences that shape our thinking and behaviour. We react differently to events with some things affecting others in a wide range of ways with sometimes no obvious reason. The fact is we are all unique and no one solution fits all. Therefore it is vital that, as much as possible, we understand ourselves and who we are. Why do we react, respond, feel, think, act and behave the way we do? Why do certain things affect us the way they do, and what can we do that will work for us? By understanding ourselves we have a much greater chance of being in control and overcoming any issues we have or will face going forward. So take the time and make the effort to really understand who you are – it will be worth it.

Your brain

Everything you do, think, say and feel and how you behave are a result of what your brain tells you. Millions of messages each day are sent inside your brain and understanding more about your brain and how it works will be very helpful to you. It is the most amazing and complex organ, but the more we understand it, the better placed we are to make the best use of it.

Having knowledge about the brain chemicals and neurotransmitters will help you make sense of some of the highs and lows you feel. Having the understanding related to the Chimp Paradox will help you make sense of your behaviour and why you do and say what you do.

Recognise any triggers

From understanding yourself better and working out how certain things will cause a negative reaction to our wellbeing, we can then do something to help ourselves. That could be to avoid the situation, person, or event. It could be to see how we can change the situation so it doesn't cause an issue; it could be to learn to try and minimise the effect it has on us; or it could be to learn how to cope better and deal with the situation or experience.

If you are aware of these 'triggers' that may cause problems then you must recognise them and put into action some kind of response that will be beneficial to you or limit any damage. Do not just let it happen or blindly ignore the triggers. Being both self-aware and aware of the triggers will allow you to be more in control and make better choices as to what you then do.

Positive vs. negative

For a long time you have probably had more negative thoughts than positive ones in your life in respect of your anxiety. You can change that. You know the difference between what is negative and what is positive, and if you focus and keep practising being positive your whole mindset will become much more positive.

Negative thinking will not help in any way. It will only compound the problems you have. You have a choice and you can choose to do, to think, to say, to feel, to behave in a positive way. You have also, most likely, had a lot more positive experiences but you have not realised or perceived them to be as positive as they were. Of course it will be hard at times and you won't feel like it, but you still have a choice. Choose to be positive and recognise the positive aspects, and it will bring positive changes to your life.

Productive vs. unproductive

In a similar way to the positive versus negative above, it is likely that you have spent a long time doing too many unproductive things rather than productive ones in relation to anxiety. Again you know the difference between the two and you have the choice as to which you take.

As much as possible do things that are productive and whenever you do, acknowledge it and give yourself a pat on the back. It's not easy to be productive when you are suffering from anxiety but it can be done and the more you do, the easier it becomes and the greater the results. Being unproductive will not just be unhelpful; it is likely to make things worse and you definitely don't want that. So keep asking yourself, "Is this productive or unproductive?" or "Do I want to feel better or not?" as they are basically the same thing.

Your defences and coping skills

You are stronger than you think and you can deal with more than you realise. You can also become even stronger and will eventually realise you can deal with anything and cope with anything. With the right tools, techniques, knowledge, and defences you are invincible. Yes, you will still have bad days and low points but going forward you will know that nothing can beat you – certainly not anxiety.

Don't become complacent, and keep working on those defences. The more you do, the more powerful and in control you become. Your confidence and self-belief will continue to increase, and the anxiety will become a thing of the past.

Stay in control – it's your ship

It is your life and it is your ship – you are the captain. You are in control of your ship and you can decide where you want to go. Keep an eye on the compass, the control panel, the satellites, etc., but also enjoy the views along your journey.

You can't do much about the weather, but if a storm does come along you now know your ship can handle it and you can do what is needed to sail through any choppy waters and you will soon have the peaceful, calm waters and blue sky with sunshine again.

Now go back through the book and the various exercises and below write down some of the most important lessons, tools and techniques you have learned or the best pieces of information and advice that will help you be the best captain you can be.

CHAPTER 8 SUMMARY

I have stated many times how important and necessary it is to apply what you have learned and to keep practising. You have all the knowledge and a wide range of tools and techniques so you can become your own expert by practising each day, so that it becomes second nature to relax, step back, be rational, think positively, realise you are in control, and be confident you can cope with anything. It will become easier and easier for you to do this as you keep practising and remind yourself of all that you have learned.

You've made it! Congratulations! I bet it has been difficult at times but the effort will be rewarded, and you deserve a lot of credit for completing the book – now enjoy being the new you.

Final thoughts

I really hope this book has been beneficial to you. I know how common anxiety is and the effect it can have on so many people, but I'm hopeful that with effort, you can overcome anxiety and as a result be happier. Please keep using this book and reread whenever you need to, as often some of the things mentioned need to be read more than once. This is your book to look at and refer to whenever you want.

I would love to hear from you with any comments or feedback, and hopefully hear how the book has helped you. Please feel free to contact me via email: info@climbyourmountain.org

Best Wishes

Charlie Wardle
Founder of Climb Your Mountain (CYM)

More from the Charity

Climb Your Mountain (CYM) was set up as a charity in 2008 with the aim of helping anyone who is going through a difficult time in their life by helping them to climb their own personal mountain. It is for anybody, any age, any background, and recognises that stress, depression, low confidence, health issues, associated conditions and lack of general wellbeing can be damaging and can affect anybody for many different reasons.

The charity has two main focuses. Firstly, there is an emphasis on using physical exercise and activities as a way of dealing with, managing, preventing and treating issues. There is a wide range of benefits to physical exercise and activities, yet it is often hard to motivate yourself, especially when you are feeling low. Also, many people are not aware of the huge benefits that physical exercise and activities can have on your mental health and wellbeing, as well as your physical health.

So the charity provides opportunities as well as encouragement and motivation for people to do more exercise and take part in more physical activities. We have organised hundreds of free walks, hikes, runs, climbs and cycle rides across the country, in a friendly and safe environment. Anyone can participate and people are there to benefit from enjoying the activities, meeting new people, seeing new places and becoming healthier and happier.

The second focus is on education and providing information and knowledge for people about physical and mental health and overall wellbeing. CYM offers free educational talks, courses and workshops that cover a wide range of topics including stress and depression (symptoms, causes, prevention, management and treatment), anxiety, brain chemistry, food and mood, benefits of exercise, confidence and self-esteem, motivation and barriers to wellbeing. There are also the self-help books that expand on the course content and can reach more people, offering practical help and advice, so they are in a better position to help themselves and to be able to help others.

Please visit the website **www.climbyourmountain.org** for more information and to get in touch. If you know of any groups, organisations or companies that would be interested in a talk or course, then get in touch.

How you can help others

We rely heavily on donations and sponsorship to fund our services, including providing these free books. If you can help us in any way or would like to volunteer or be involved, then you can help many other people. Please get in touch!

We also organise overseas treks and challenges as fundraising events for the charity with trips such as Kilimanjaro, Everest Base Camp trek, Pyrenees Thousand Lakes trek, Mount Toubkal, Great Wall of China trek, the Inca Trail and others. So again, if interested, get in touch!

Please email info@climbyourmountain.org
Or go to the website www.climbyourmountain.org

Outdoor adventures & challenges

My main business away from the charity is organising outdoor trips, adventures and challenges, and you may be interested to see what is on offer. The website is **www.themountaincoach.com**

There is a wide range of UK trips, challenges and adventures for all levels including open events for the public and private groups. A great way to enjoy the outdoors, see new places, keep fit and healthy, boost your confidence, meet new people, make new friends, and generally have a great time!

Company talks, workshops & seminars on Health & Wellbeing

In addition, I can deliver talks, workshops and seminars on a wide range of 'Health & Wellbeing' topics to groups, organisations and companies through the Climb Your Mountain charity.

If interested, please get in touch via:

Email: info@climbyourmountain.org

Website: www.climbyourmountain.org